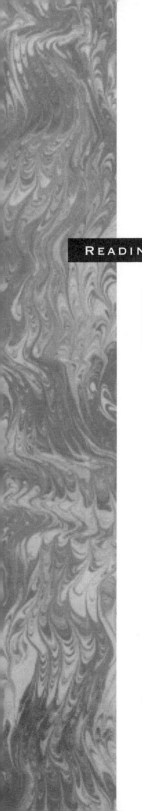

# ERNEST HEMINGWAY

THE GREENHAVEN PRESS

*Literary Companion*

TO AMERICAN AUTHORS

READINGS ON

# ERNEST HEMINGWAY

David Bender, *Publisher*

Bruno Leone, *Executive Editor*

Scott Barbour, *Managing Editor*

Bonnie Szumski, *Series Editor*

Katie de Koster, *Book Editor*

Greenhaven Press, San Diego, CA

Library of Congress Cataloging-in-Publication Data

Readings on Ernest Hemingway / Katie de Koster, book editor.
     p.      cm. — (Greenhaven Press literary companion
to American authors)
   Includes bibliographical references and index.
   ISBN 1-56510-463-3 (lib. : alk. paper). —
ISBN 1-56510-462-5 (pbk. : alk. paper)
   1. Hemingway, Ernest, 1899–1961—Criticism and interpretation. I. de Koster, Katie, 1948–   . II. Series.
PS3515.E37Z75455   1997
813'.52–dc20                                    96-21137
                                                    CIP

Copyright ©1997 by Greenhaven Press, Inc.
PO Box 289009
San Diego, CA 92198-9009
Printed in the U.S.A.

*"If a writer of prose knows enough about what he is writing about he may omit things that he knows and the reader, if the writer is writing truly enough, will have a feeling of those things as strongly as though the writer had stated them. The dignity of movement of an iceberg is due to only one-eighth of it being above water."*

*Ernest Hemingway*
**Death in the Afternoon**

# CONTENTS

# Chapter 2: Hemingway: The Man in His Work

# Chapter 3: The Hemingway Style

Hemingway's treatment of food in his writing illustrates his "iceberg principle," his theory that as long as a writer *knows* everything about his scenes and characters, he only need *show* a small part to be credible. His use of specific, concrete information about food is also an example of his insistence on using "true" information to invest his writing with impact, immediacy, and authority.

# Chapter 4: Hemingway Reconsidered

Although he exhibits sympathy for the plight of women in this novel, Hemingway consistently devalues Cubans and Africans, using them as foils to increase the perceived stature of the white hero.

# FOREWORD

*"'Tis the good reader that
makes the good book."*

Ralph Waldo Emerson

The story's bare facts are simple: The captain, an old and scarred seafarer, walks with a peg leg made of whale ivory. He relentlessly drives his crew to hunt the world's oceans for the great white whale that crippled him. After a long search, the ship encounters the whale and a fierce battle ensues. Finally the captain drives his harpoon into the whale, but the harpoon line catches the captain about the neck and drags him to his death.

A simple story, a straightforward plot—yet, since the 1851 publication of Herman Melville's *Moby-Dick*, readers and critics have found many meanings in the struggle between Captain Ahab and the whale. To some, the novel is a cautionary tale that depicts how Ahab's obsession with revenge leads to his insanity and death. Others believe that the whale represents the unknowable secrets of the universe and that Ahab is a tragic hero who dares to challenge fate by attempting to discover this knowledge. Perhaps Melville intended Ahab as a criticism of Americans' tendency to become involved in well-intentioned but irrational causes. Or did Melville model Ahab after himself, letting his fictional character express his anger at what he perceived as a cruel and distant god?

Although literary critics disagree over the meaning of *Moby-Dick*, readers do not need to choose one particular interpretation in order to gain an understanding of Melville's novel. Instead, by examining various analyses, they can gain numerous insights into the issues that lie under the surface of the basic plot. Studying the writings of literary critics can also aid readers in making their own assessments of *Moby-Dick* and other literary works and in developing analytical thinking skills.

The Greenhaven Literary Companion Series was created with these goals in mind. Designed for young adults, this unique anthology series provides an engaging and comprehensive introduction to literary analysis and criticism. The essays included in the Literary Companion Series are chosen for their accessibility to a young adult audience and are expertly edited in consideration of both the reading and comprehension levels of this audience. In addition, each essay is introduced by a concise summation that presents the contributing writer's main themes and insights. Every anthology in the Literary Companion Series contains a varied selection of critical essays that cover a wide time span and express diverse views. Wherever possible, primary sources are represented through excerpts from authors' notebooks, letters, and journals and through contemporary criticism.

Each title in the Literary Companion Series pays careful consideration to the historical context of the particular author or literary work. In-depth biographies and detailed chronologies reveal important aspects of authors' lives and emphasize the historical events and social milieu that influenced their writings. To facilitate further research, every anthology includes primary and secondary source bibliographies of articles and/or books selected for their suitability for young adults. These engaging features make the Greenhaven Literary Companion series ideal for introducing students to literary analysis in the classroom or as a library resource for young adults researching the world's great authors and literature.

Exceptional in its focus on young adults, the Greenhaven Literary Companion Series strives to present literary criticism in a compelling and accessible format. Every title in the series is intended to spark readers' interest in leading American and world authors, to help them broaden their understanding of literature, and to encourage them to formulate their own analyses of the literary works that they read. It is the editors' hope that young adult readers will find these anthologies to be true companions in their study of literature.

# INTRODUCTION

Often when an author dies, material that was kept private or hidden during his or her lifetime is revealed. So it was with Hemingway. He tried to suppress the efforts of biographers, even threatened to withdraw financial support from his mother if she cooperated with anyone who wanted to write about his childhood. When he failed to suppress a biographical effort entirely, he would occasionally offer minimal cooperation to try to control what was learned and what was said about him. During his lifetime, his efforts were fairly successful; after his death, volumes of material—including books written by family members (notably his least-favorite sister, Marcelline Hemingway Sanford)—became available to those who wanted to write about the author behind the work.

One thing biographers do is debunk. Recent major biographers (e.g., Kenneth S. Lynn and James R. Mellow) have had access not only to the work of their predecessors and memoirs of family and friends but also to official records that have gradually become available (or have been unearthed by the researchers) over the years. These writers have dismantled many of the myths Hemingway spun around himself. Like one of his own favorite authors, Samuel L. Clemens/Mark Twain, Hemingway had created a persona for himself that was both part of and an extension of his fiction. Those who knew Hemingway during his lifetime often repeated his tales as fact, contributing to the building of a larger-than-life icon of an author. Today's view is a bit more life-size: He was an enormously talented man with problems. During Hemingway's lifetime, heroes were popular; now, at the end of the twentieth century, people tend to distrust heroes.

These changing views are reflected not just in biographical works but also in the literary commentary that has been written over the years. For example, writing in 1940, Edgar Johnson finds a new kind of hopefulness in *To Have and*

*Have Not.* Johnson was writing as World War II engulfed Europe. Much of the analysis written by Hemingway's contemporaries relates to how he interpreted the world they had in common, or how they interpret his interpretation.

Commentaries written within a few years after Hemingway died tend to be heavily colored by the fact of his suicide. For example, in writing about *A Farewell to Arms* in 1967, Stanley Cooperman charged that Hemingway feared "the full spectrum of experience," a conclusion he felt was proven by the manner of his death. Since Hemingway had written so often of the necessity of facing death with courage—"grace under pressure," as he called it—many struggled to fit the final act of self-destruction into what seemed to be a contrary philosophy.

Many later writers, on the other hand, focus on *how* he did what he did, his literary technique and the influences on his style. (For example, his short sentences have been variously credited to the influence of the *Kansas City Star*, Gertrude Stein, and the telegraphic style developed in reporting by wire, among others.) Others apply today's politically correct standards and often find Hemingway wanting in such areas as anti-Semitism and treatment of women and minorities. Arguments abound over what the author "meant" when he wrote; an example is the controversy over the portrayal of the main characters in *The Sun Also Rises.* James Twitchell and Charles Child Walcutt examine the same text and come to very different conclusions, a common occurrence in the literary world.

All of these points of view are represented in the writings in this volume. They help to illustrate that like most forms of knowledge, literary analysis continually changes. It would be unwise to accept any single point of view as "the truth" about Hemingway, but all of them together can contribute to a well-rounded understanding of the writer's art.

# ERNEST HEMINGWAY: A BIOGRAPHY

Ernest Hemingway gazes out from the covers of two hefty literary biographies. On one, a passport photo shows a young man in his late teens, intense, assertive, self-confident (a bit cocky?), clean-shaven, good-looking. On the other, a somewhat grizzled man of about sixty, gray hair and beard a bit shaggy, seems to be slightly confused, unsure of himself, vulnerable. The first photo is of a young man who had yet to make his mark; the second, the winner of numerous literary awards including the Pulitzer and Nobel prizes—the Grand Old Man of Literature—who would commit suicide not long after the photo was taken.

Taking his own life cast a long shadow back over Hemingway's accomplishments. Most literary (and personal) analyses since his death in 1961 have been colored by the fact of his self-destruction, and several biographers have tried to understand how that cocky young man, after achieving more than most men ever dream, became the unhappy man of his last years. Many find some of the seeds of sadness in the relationship between his mother and his father, and in his relationships with them.

## GRACE AND CLARENCE HEMINGWAY

Grace Hall Hemingway, Ernest's mother, was the daughter and granddaughter of strong-willed women, and she was raised to think highly of herself. She had chafed under the restrictions placed on girls when she was growing up and had in fact been a bit of a tomboy. (She rode her brother's bicycle down the street, a caper considered shocking at the time.) Hemingway biographer Kenneth S. Lynn says she was a "gifted, charming, physically impressive woman." Trained for a career in music, she failed to become a premier soprano when she had a traumatic debut at New York City's

Madison Square Garden in 1896. (The circumstances have been variously reported, but she apparently was unable to perform under the bright lights of the stage.) Giving up her dream, as she put it, she consented to marry Clarence Hemingway, a young doctor who had helped treat her mother at home during her final illness.

The Hemingways lived near Chicago in Oak Park, Illinois, a community that considered itself above the norm according to such standards as culture and social caste. Grace had no problem beginning a second career there, earning her own money as a music teacher. (In the early years of their marriage, she made more than Clarence did.) In a society that was just beginning to consider women as no longer completely ruled by men (although women would still not be allowed to vote in national elections until 1920), Grace refused to play a traditional, subservient role. She ignored Clarence's edicts when she chose to; for example, she caused quite a strain in the relationship when she insisted on purchasing a second vacation home for her personal use near the family's longtime summer home in Michigan. (She once warned Ernest, after Clarence had died, "Never threaten me with what to do. Your father tried that once when we were first married and he lived to regret it.") Ernest and other family members remembered times when she had humiliated Clarence in public, which he seems generally to have taken in stoic silence. Grace also considered it beneath her to do the cooking and housework, so it frequently fell to her husband to tend to domestic life after he returned home from work. It seems likely that Clarence suffered from a form of depression, which may have made him less able to cope with such a relationship. At any rate, when Clarence committed suicide in 1928, Ernest blamed his mother.

## "TWINS"

Grace and Clarence's first child, Marcelline, was born January 15, 1898. Oddly, after Ernest Miller Hemingway was born some eighteen months later, on July 21, 1899, Grace insisted on treating the two children as if they were twins. Ernest was often clothed in dresses like Marcelline's—a custom that was not too odd at the time. But his mother also occasionally referred to him as her "beautiful girl" or "summer girl."

Grace had Marcelline's schooling delayed so she and Ernest could enter school together, as the "twins" they were supposed to be. Since Marcelline was a year and a half older than her brother, she was more advanced both physically and intellectually during the several years they were schooled together. Treating Ernest and Marcelline alike may have been Grace's attempt to give her daughter the equality she had wanted for herself, but for Ernest it added a frustrating element to the inevitable sibling rivalry.

## AN ORDINARY CHILDHOOD

Ernest would eventually have four sisters and a brother. The outer trappings of the Hemingway children's childhood were those of a fairly privileged middle-class family. Grace regularly took her children on culturally enriching treks to nearby Chicago. Summers were spent at Windemere, the family's cottage on Walloon Lake in Michigan, where Clarence shared with his son his considerable proficiency in fishing, hunting, and other outdoor skills.

Oak Park was a religious community, and the routine piety of the Hemingway family fitted the town's norm. Prayer and Bible readings were part of the Hemingways' daily routine, and a strict observance of rules both secular and religious was required. Drinking, like dancing, was a sin. Ernest seems to have been an obedient son for the most part, and a repentant one when he strayed.

Yet there were signs of the determinedly self-defined man he would become. Hemingway biographer Carlos Baker notes that Ernest learned to box in 1916; he adds, "There was a streak of the bully in his nature which began to emerge when he learned of the power in his fists." In 1940 his editor, Maxwell Perkins, related an anecdote in which he discerned Ernest's boyhood persistence and courage:

> One of the earliest stories significant of his character I do know to be fact. When he was still a boy, but large for his age and strong, his father, yielding to his urgency, gave him the price of an advertised course in boxing. You paid the ex-fighter in advance and he turned you over to a pug. In the first lesson young Hemingway got rough treatment. His nose was broken. Few returned for a second lesson, but Hemingway did, and he finished the course. It never even occurred to him that this was a racket—that you weren't supposed to come back ever.

That determination to face fear and pain found expression in Hemingway's "code of the hero." The code would become an important part of his writing, and of his life. So, to a lesser extent, would his tendency to be a bully.

## JOURNALISM VS. WAR

A few months after he graduated from high school in June 1917, his uncle Alfred Tyler Hemingway helped him get a job as a cub reporter with the *Kansas City Star*. This seems to have been a compromise with his parents: they wanted him to go to college, and he wanted to volunteer to help fight the war against Germany. (The United States had just entered World War I in April of that year.)

Ernest spent several months at the *Star*, learning on the job about the newspaper trade. His boss, C.G. Wellington, gave him the newspaper's style sheet and told him to memorize—and apply—the long list of dos and don'ts: "Use short sentences. Use short first paragraphs. Use vigorous English. Be positive, not negative." He would later say these were "the best rules" he had ever learned for writing.

But he still wanted to go to war. By early 1918, when Italian Red Cross officials arrived in Kansas City on a recruitment drive, he was eager to sign up. (The Red Cross was only allowed to recruit men who could not be drafted; Hemingway had defective vision in his left eye.) When he was accepted, he gave his notice to the *Star*, leaving the paper at the end of April 1918. Ernest's parents (especially his father, who had hoped his son would also become a doctor) approved this "useful Christian service" and gave their blessing to his plans.

## THE "FIRST" AMERICAN CASUALTY

On June 7, 1918, his first day at his new post in Milan, Italy, a munitions factory exploded and Hemingway was one of those dispatched to help. The factory was surrounded by bodies and splattered with bits and pieces of people, including fragments of flesh caught by its heavy barbed wire fencing. Fourteen years later his memories of the scene would form the basis of the section in *Death in the Afternoon* called "A Natural History of the Dead."

As fighting shifted to the south, Hemingway volunteered to man a relief station behind the lines at Fossalta di Piave; his duties would include bringing chocolate and cigarettes to the Italian soldiers at the front. In the middle of the night on July 8, Hemingway was delivering supplies near the front lines when he was hit by shrapnel from a trench mortar shell. He was seriously wounded in the head and both legs—although not as seriously (in number or severity of wounds) as his later war-tale exaggerations would have it. Early biographers took those claims as fact, along with tales of a heroic attempt to save an Italian soldier who had been mortally wounded by the same shell. Most later biographers (who had access to more records) believe that the fictional account of Lieutenant Henry's wounding in *A Farewell to Arms* comes closer to the truth of Hemingway's experience. In the book Lieutenant Rinaldi says, "They want to get you the medaglia d'argento. ... Did you do any heroic act? ... Didn't you carry anybody on your back?" And Henry responds, "I didn't carry anyone. I couldn't move."

However, as Kenneth Lynn observes, "when it came to handing out medals to their allies, ... Italy's military commanders were proverbially generous." Hemingway—like Henry—was awarded the Italian Silver Medal.

Celebrated as the first American casualty of the war (although a fellow ambulance driver had been killed by Austrian fire a few weeks earlier), Hemingway and his wounds received a great deal of attention from the press. His sister Marcelline was watching a newsreel in a Chicago movie theater when he suddenly appeared onscreen, shown in a wheelchair at a Milan hospital.

Hemingway had been transferred from a field hospital to that hospital in Milan just four days before his nineteenth birthday. With eighteen nurses for a half-dozen wounded soldiers, patients received plenty of attention. One of his nurses, twenty-six-year-old Agnes von Kurowsky, a librarian from Washington, D.C., became his first serious crush. (At least one biographer noted similarities between Agnes and Hemingway's mother. Kenneth Lynn writes, "At five feet eight inches tall, Agnes was the same height as Grace and her chestnut hair was almost exactly the same color.")

After several months of recuperation and with the war over (as of November 11), Hemingway returned to the United States to a hero's welcome. He had proposed to Agnes and she had hinted that her answer might be yes. He planned to get a job and establish a home for them, and he was crushed and angered when he received a letter from her saying she had found someone else. Some of the anger shows in the tenth sketch in his second book, *in our time*, published in Paris: A nurse named Ag, who meets the wounded-soldier hero in a hospital in Milan and agrees to marry him, throws him over after he returns to the States, writing him that "theirs had been only a boy affair." (Hemingway also included a longer version of the vignette, titled "A Very Short Story," in his first book published in the United States, *In Our Time*. He changed the nurse's name and the locations for the second and later editions of the American version.) A more complex reworking of fact into fiction is found in the relationship between Frederick Henry and Catherine Barkley in *A Farewell to Arms*, in which the relationship holds firm but the heroine dies.

Back at home with his parents, Ernest initially took to his bed with a fever on receiving Ms. von Kurowsky's rejection. But he was soon working hard at writing short stories. Since these were invariably rejected by the magazines he sent them to, his mother became increasingly frustrated with him: he would not go to college, would not get a job, and would not even clean up his messy room. On his part, Ernest was furious that after all he had experienced and suffered, his mother still treated him as a boy. His mother's failure to treat him with what he felt was the proper respect was in vivid contrast to his treatment by the other residents of Oak Park, who often invited him to civic gatherings to speak about his experiences in the war and celebrated him as their own war hero.

Ernest accompanied his family to Michigan that summer, but he stayed mostly with friends. His mother complained that he was seldom around to do chores for her. When the family returned to Oak Park in the fall, he stayed in Michigan, renting a room in a boardinghouse in Petoskey and trying to make a living as a freelance fiction writer. In December he was invited to give his popular war-experiences lecture for the benefit of the Petoskey Ladies Aid Society. His dramatic tale impressed the audience, whose members included Harriet Connable, wife of the head of the F.W. Woolworth chain in Canada. The Connables offered Hemingway a job as companion to their son at their home in Toronto while they spent a winter vacation in Florida. To sweeten the deal, Ralph Connable promised to introduce the young writer to his friends at the *Toronto Star Weekly*. He accepted. His first article for the newspaper was published on February 14, 1920, and fifteen more articles followed in the next three or four months. At the Connables' insistence, he stayed on with them when the rest of the family returned from their vacation, but by late spring he was ready to return to Michigan.

Ernest was looking forward to a summer of fishing and loafing; his parents expected him to make himself useful around the summerhouse. By July his parents had become increasingly concerned. Not only had he refused to cooperate in their plans for him, he had become belligerent. Clarence, who was in Oak Park for most of the summer, had sent him five dollars to do some spraying; he kept the money but did not do the chore. On July 21, 1920, Ernest was twenty-one years old. Shortly after his birthday dinner at Windemere, his parents told him to stay away from the family home until he was invited.

Adding to the crisis was a secret midnight outing that two of Ernest's sisters and some of their friends decided to have on the night of July 26. The Hemingway girls, Ursula and Sunny, had persuaded Ernest and his friend Brummy (Ted Brumback) to come along as chaperones. When the empty beds were discovered, the two men were blamed. The affair was an innocent one, but the involvement of their neighbors made the situation worse: Mrs. Loomis, mother of two of the truant children, announced that "she would pack up and take her whole family back to Oak Park unless we could do something to get rid of those grown men loafing around." When Grace confronted her son, she told Clarence,

> Of course Ernest called me every name he could think of, and said everything vile about me.... Oh! But he is a cruel son. ... [He] said "all I read is moron literature,"... and asked me if I read the *Atlantic Monthly* just so someone would see me doing it.... He is distinctly a menace to youth.

Clarence was also sorrowed and outraged by his son. He wrote Grace, "He must get busy and make his own way, and suffering alone will be the means of softening his Iron Heart of selfishness."

For his part, Ernest portrayed himself as very put-upon and misjudged, claiming that he had done the work of a "hired man" that summer. He deeply resented both his parents' expectations and their treatment of him. But, as James Mellow notes, "Clarence and Grace had stuck to their principles, as they had been brought up to do in a world of values that were fading. And Hemingway, unable to forgive his father for being the man he was, reserved his scorn for his mother, whom he blamed for all the trouble."

## ON HIS OWN

Hemingway decided to move to Chicago. There, in October 1920, he met Elizabeth Hadley Richardson. He later claimed to his brother, Leicester, that as soon as Hadley entered the room, "an intense feeling came over me. I knew she was the girl I was going to marry." And so he did, on September 3, 1921.

After a honeymoon at Windemere (he had achieved a wary reconciliation with his parents), the newlyweds were off to France. Hemingway was to be the *Toronto Daily Star*'s foreign correspondent in Europe.

Ernest had met Sherwood Anderson, a popular novelist, at the Chicago Men's Club. Anderson, recently back from France, had provided the Hemingways with letters of introduction to several important people there, including writers Gertrude Stein and Ezra Pound, and Lewis Galantière, an American translator and writer who was well versed in French culture.

Galantière promptly invited the new arrivals to have dinner with him and his girlfriend. At dinner Hemingway challenged the translator to come back to the hotel for a little sparring. Catching him when his guard was down, Hemingway delivered a blow to the face that broke Galantière's glasses. It made an awkward end to the evening. (Over the years Hemingway would similarly challenge many other men—critics, authors, drinking buddies, a suitor of one of his sisters—men usually smaller than him, and nearly always less experienced in boxing. It was a peculiar and unattractive form of bullying that was seldom the "sportsmanlike" encounter he claimed.)

Fortunately the introduction to Gertrude Stein went more smoothly. Stein invited Hadley and Ernest to join her and her companion, Alice B. Toklas, for tea, and after that first meeting Stein and Hemingway developed a warm friendship. It was Stein who supplied the term Hemingway made famous in *The Sun Also Rises*, "the Lost Generation." ("All of you young people who served in the war. You are a lost generation.")

Hemingway also hit it off with Ezra Pound. Pound asked to see some of Hemingway's work, and quickly pronounced his poems "swell" and sent them off to *The Dial* in New York. They were rejected, as was the story Pound had proposed to publish in *The Little Review*, but the fact that he had made the effort bolstered Hemingway's belief in his own writing.

## FOREIGN CORRESPONDENT

The Hemingways met many other writers and artists in Paris, and Ernest was working on poems and short stories with great dedication. But he also had a job. Even though he complained, after only three months in Paris, that "this goddam newspaper stuff is gradually ruining me," it was his position as a correspondent for the *Toronto Star* that paid the bills.

Reporting for the *Star* sent him traveling around Europe. He covered the 1922 International Economic Conference in Genoa, Italy, where his economic analysis was spotty but his descriptions of personalities and the rise of Fascism vivid. He and Hadley vacationed in Germany; he wrote articles on German inflation and the hostility of Germans toward those who benefited from the devalued German mark, and on the riot of a German mob protesting the high cost of living. In September 1922 the *Star* sent him to cover the last stages of the Greco-Turkish war. He wrote of Constantinople in panic, of the evacuation of the Greek army, of a twenty-mile column of refugees in bullock-drawn carts and of a woman giving birth in one of them as her frightened daughter watched. Then—after a brief trip back to Paris and Hadley—he was off to Lausanne, Switzerland, to report on the conference that would try to settle the territorial disputes between the Greeks and Turks. Here, just months after having written glowingly of Mussolini's rise to power (he had interviewed the Fascist Italian leader in Milan), he reversed his opinion and wrote scathingly of a man he now considered a fraud.

## BUMBY

An unexpected event was soon to change the Hemingways' life: Hadley became pregnant. The couple would return to Toronto for the baby's birth. Hemingway managed to fit in a trip to Spain before they left; he had picked up on Stein's enthusiasm for the bullfight as ritual and was eager to see the confrontation of matador and toro in person. His passion for the spectacle would be illustrated some nine years later, in *Death in the Afternoon*, as well as in short stories and articles.

Another project to be completed before he left: checking the proofs and cover design for his first book, *Three Stories and Ten Poems*, which Robert McAlmon was publishing in Paris. Hemingway was also writing and revising vignettes for his second book published in Paris, *in our time*. (One of the new pieces was on the fictionalized death of a matador he had just seen and admired in Pamplona.)

Toronto, after Paris, was boring. He was working for the *Daily Star*, being sent out on what Hadley called "absurd assignments," often until two in the morning, by a boss who did not like him. He was away on assignment in New York when Hadley went into labor; their son, John Hadley Nicanor Hemingway, was born on October 11, 1922. (The infant was quickly nicknamed Bumby. In later years, he would be known as Jack to those who watched his television show on fishing.) Among the Christmas gifts Grace Hemingway would send her new grandson: a short dress like the ones in which she had dressed his father.

Having been sent out of town by his hated boss when Hadley was about to deliver led to a blowup at the office, and Hemingway was soon working exclusively for the *Weekly Star*, back under his old, more agreeable boss, J. Herbert Cranston. The feature stories he was writing now gave him more time to promote his first two books, but he was still itchy to return to Europe. He quit his job, and by mid-January the young Hemingway family was headed back to France.

## PARIS, AGAIN

When *in our time* was finally published, Edmund Wilson reviewed both of Hemingway's books in *The Dial*. Wilson wrote that Hemingway, Stein, and Sherwood Anderson now could be considered a school, distinguished by "a naiveté of language, often passing into the colloquialism of the character dealt with, which serves actually to convey profound emotions and complex states of minds. It is a distinctively American development in prose." Although Hemingway would later work to dissociate himself from Stein and Anderson, he was grateful for the warm review.

He was already working on another book, his first to be published in the United States. *In Our Time* would include fourteen stories, interwoven with vignettes (including those from the Paris book, *in our time*). Calling it a masterpiece, James Mellow writes:

> Through the character of Nick Adams, the hero of many (though not all) of the stories of *In Our Time*, Hemingway created a fictional persona for himself and for his time. He an-

nounced themes that would carry him through a lifetime of
work: the disappointments of family life, the disaffections of
early love, the celebration of country and male comradeship,
a young man's initiation into the world of sex, the consequences of marriage. In the interchapters, Hemingway recre-
ated the destructive violence of battle and the ritual violence
of bullfighting intended to give the larger chronicle of his
times—the world of war and politics, of crime and punish-
ment—that were juxtaposed with the more personal circumstances of the stories.

Hemingway's friend Don Stewart had been trying to find
an American publisher for *In Our Time*, and finally succeeded in getting Boni and Liveright to offer a contract,
which included an option for his next two books. Sherwood
Anderson, who had just switched publishers to B & L, wrote
a blurb of unqualified praise for the cover of the book.

## A CAREER LAUNCHED

*In Our Time*, Hemingway's American fiction debut, received
some enthusiastic reviews. But Hemingway was not happy.
Many reviewers compared his work with that of Stein and
Anderson, and he did not like the comparison. In fact, the
identification with Anderson (compounded by his friend's
enthusiastic blurb on the book's cover) drove Hemingway to
write *The Torrents of Spring*, a scathing parody of Anderson's novel *Dark Laughter*. Banging it out in ten days, he decided to use it for a dual purpose: not only would it emphasize the separation between them, he would use it to get out
of his contract with Boni and Liveright so he could publish
with Max Perkins, F. Scott Fitzgerald's editor at Scribner's.
(In his opinion, B & L was not sufficiently enthusiastic about
his work.) The ruse worked. B & L would not publish a work
so mean-spirited and harmful to another of their own authors, and refused to exercise their option. Hemingway joy-
fully turned to Perkins.

*The Torrents of Spring* was Hemingway's first book for
Scribner's. Several biographers have found in it more than a
parody of Anderson. A tale of a triangle between a man and
two women that ends with the man's feeling empty as he
gets the "new" woman, it echoes what was going on in Hemingway's life while he was writing it. Pauline Pfeiffer, an editor at the Paris office of *Vogue*, had decided she wanted
Hemingway for herself. After a protracted chase, she got him:
Hemingway somewhat sadly asked Hadley for a divorce.

## FAMILY REACTIONS

Hemingway had earlier had six copies of *in our time* sent to his parents; his father, disgusted by the subject matter, had returned them to the publisher. Now, with the breakup of his marriage to Hadley, hints of alcoholism, and the publication of *The Sun Also Rises*, family tensions again came into the open. His parents were glad to see him successful, they wrote, but surely he could use his God-given talent to a higher purpose. Grace considered it a doubtful honor to have written "one of the filthiest books of the year"—her opinion of *The Sun Also Rises*. Despite the very favorable tone of the major critical reviews, she encouraged him to mend his ways: "I love you dear, and still believe you will do something worthwhile to live after you."

Hemingway fired off an angry response, accusing his mother of hypocrisy. The book was no more offensive than "the real inner lives of some of our best Oak Park families," he said, in a veiled reference to his own family life. He later wrote his father:

> I *know* that I am not disgracing you in my writing but rather doing something that some day you will be proud of. . . . You could if you wanted be proud of me sometimes. . . . You cannot know how it makes me feel for Mother to be ashamed of what I know as sure as you know that there is a God in heaven is *not to be ashamed of.*

Yet just one month later *Men Without Women* would be published by Scribner's. As Kenneth Lynn notes, the last story in the book, " 'Now I Lay Me,'. . . with its devastating portrait of Grace, was bound to bring shame to her."

## FAREWELL THE STARVING ARTIST

While his parents did not appreciate his work, publishers, critics, and the reading public did. When *The Sun Also Rises* came out in October 1926, the first printing quickly sold out. And then the second, and soon the third. *Scribner's Magazine* and *Atlantic Monthly* now sent checks instead of rejection letters. At the same time, Pauline's wealthy family helped the couple pay their expenses—her uncle Gus Pfeiffer, for example, offered to pay the rent on a nice apartment in Paris for the two of them, and other relatives sent thousand-dollar checks as wedding gifts. With *Men Without Women* scheduled for the fall of 1927, Hemingway abandoned his pride in his scruffy appearance and treated himself to some fancy new clothes.

He could afford to indulge his tastes on a much more expensive scale now. When Pauline announced she was pregnant and did not want to have her baby in Europe, Hemingway began looking around for a new base of operations.

## KEY WEST

In March 1928 Pauline and "Papa," as Hemingway now liked to be called, moved to Key West, Florida, where he set to work on *A Farewell to Arms*.

Hemingway discovered that his parents were vacationing in Florida and invited them to join him and Pauline. Grace was in robust health, but his father had deteriorated alarmingly. Plagued by diabetes and angina attacks and distressed by the failures of his land investments in Florida, he made a shocking contrast to his vibrant, self-satisfied wife.

Pauline had decided to have her baby in Kansas City, so it was there that Hemingway continued work on *A Farewell to Arms*. On June 17, he wrote a friend that he knew how the novel was going to end. Eerily, ten days later his second son, Patrick, was delivered, after a long labor, by Caesarean section—an event similar to the end of the novel. But while Pauline survived childbirth, the fictional Catherine Barkley did not.

On December 6, Hemingway picked up his five-year-old son, Bumby, at the New York dock for his annual visit and boarded a train for Key West. At Trenton, New Jersey, he was handed a telegram saying his father had died that morning. He sent his son on to Key West in care of a porter and headed for Oak Park, where he learned his father had committed suicide.

Clarence had awakened that day with a pain in his foot, and before long he had decided it would lead to gangrene and amputation. (As a physician, he knew this was a common complication of diabetes. Added to his other physical, mental, and financial woes, it must have seemed too much to bear.) He killed himself around noon. His thirteen-year-old son, Leicester, heard the shot and found the body. (Those sounds and sights haunted Leicester—Ernest's only brother—for the rest of his life. In 1982, told that he would have to have his legs amputated because of diabetes, he too shot himself.)

Shaken by his father's suicide, Hemingway returned to Key West to rework, over and over, the ending of *A Farewell to Arms*. When it was finally published in September 1929, sales were brisk, and continued so even after the collapse of the stock market and the resulting financial panic in October. The reviews were superlative; from the royalties for this book he set up a trust fund for his mother to supplement the allowance he had begun sending her.

The Hemingways had been renting places in Key West for a couple of years, but in 1931 they settled into their own home. Pauline had fallen in love with a house on Whitehead Street, and her uncle Gus had purchased it for her as a gift. There Hemingway worked on a few short stories and on his bullfighting book, *Death in the Afternoon*, with a trip to Spain that spring and summer to take in the bullfights and evaluate the new bullfighters. While he was there, he observed the political unrest in the country, which would soon lead to civil war.

On November 12, 1931, Gregory Hancock Hemingway, Ernest and Pauline's second son (his third; he kept hoping for a daughter) was born. Like Patrick's it was a difficult Caesarean birth, and Pauline's doctor warned her not to conceive again. In April 1932 Hemingway "fled from the sound of a squalling infant" (as biographer Lynn puts it), heading for Havana for two weeks. He stayed for two months, marlin fishing in the mornings and working on *Death* galley proofs and another Nick Adams short story in the afternoons.

In September 1932 *Death in the Afternoon* was published. Initial reviews were mixed but generally positive.

## ROAMING THE WORLD

Although he professed himself happy in Key West, by 1933 Hemingway was planning to spend several months in Havana for fishing, followed by a trip to Spain and an African safari. (Uncle Gus had offered to finance the $25,000 cost of the safari.)

In Spain he found both the bullfights and the new republic disappointing (he predicted another revolution). From there he joined Pauline in Paris, where it seemed all the news of old friends was depressing and everyone talked calmly about "the next war." While he was in Paris, Max Perkins sent him the early reviews for his latest collection of stories, *Winner Take Nothing*; critics called the book his worst writing and suggested that he was losing his ability to write. He was also unhappy with Scribner's for not properly promoting *Death in the Afternoon.*

After these depressing sojourns, Africa was a treat. Hemingway had contracted to write a series of "letters" for a new magazine, *Esquire.* In his first missive from Africa he wrote, "Nothing that I have ever read or seen has given any idea of the beauty of the country or the still remaining quantity of game." He would address that deficiency with *Green Hills of Africa* (which he misleadingly called "absolutely true autobiography") and short stories, especially "The Snows of Kilimanjaro" and "The Short Happy Life of Francis Macomber."

On returning to New York, Hemingway decided to buy a sleek power boat, to be delivered to him in Florida. He named it the *Pilar,* after the code name Pauline had used during their affair while he was still married to Hadley. But Pauline was not often invited to join the excursions on her namesake.

*Green Hills of Africa* was published in October 1935. Since Uncle Gus had paid for the safari that provided the material for the book, Pauline was treated so well in the book that one reviewer commented on the "delicacy of his love for his wife." Other reviews were less approving. By December Hemingway had entered a deep depression.

## Spanish Civil War

When civil war broke out in Spain in the middle of 1936, Hemingway was eager to be on the scene. When the North American Newspaper Alliance (NANA), a news service, asked him if he'd like to become a war correspondent again, he jumped at the chance. He would visit the country four times, in the spring and fall of 1937 and of 1938.

His marriage was deteriorating, so he was happy to get away from Pauline when he went to Spain ... but he did not like to be alone. He found a solution in Martha (Marty) Gellhorn, a journalist and author whose works had been compared, not unfavorably, to his own. They first met in December 1936 in Sloppy Joe's Bar in Key West. They shared a suite in Madrid during his first trip there, in spring 1937, and with his help she became an excellent war correspondent. (Unfortunately, his own reportorial skills were less stellar; NANA eventually dropped him as a correspondent.) And just as *The Torrents of Spring,* written while he was poised between Hadley and Pauline, foretold an unhappy end to the choices he would make, *The Fifth Column,* which he was writing "between" Pauline and Marty, foretold another marital mistake. (The three-act play would be published in 1938 in *The Fifth Column and the First Forty-Nine Stories.*)

He found himself more productive in Havana than in Key West, so he was often in Cuba during the summer of 1939. Marty Gellhorn was there, too; Pauline had decided to spend the summer in Europe. Marty had found and renovated an old farmhouse, the Finca Vigía, and Hemingway had moved in with her. He had put aside his novel *For Whom the Bell Tolls* until he learned how the Spanish war would turn out; now he returned to it, trying feverishly to finish it before war broke out in Europe. Before it was published in October 1940, World War II was well under way. The book was a runaway best-seller, with nearly half a million copies sold during the first six months after publication.

## Marriage, Again. And Again.

Hemingway's divorce from Pauline and his marriage to Marty took place two weeks apart, in November 1940. Their honeymoon was an Oriental tour covering the Sino-Japanese War, she writing for *Collier's*, he for a new liberal daily, *PM*. They parted in Rangoon; she continued the tour (Singapore, Dutch East Indies), while he was eager to return to Cuba.

Back in Cuba, he volunteered the guesthouse of the Finca Vigía as the headquarters of a counterintelligence unit he would set up ("the Crook Factory") and the thirty-eight-foot *Pilar*, armed with bazookas and grenades, as a one-ship antisub task force. A friend at the American embassy got the American ambassador, Spruille Braden, to consider the plans. At Braden's request, the Cuban government authorized both the Crook Factory and the sub hunting.

While Hemingway roamed the Caribbean looking for subs, Marty accepted hazardous assignments in England, North Africa, and Italy in 1943 and 1944. This was not Hemingway's idea of wifely duties, especially since she was being highly paid for her reporting (while he was not). He sent her angry cablegrams ("ARE YOU A WAR CORRESPONDENT OR WIFE IN MY BED"). As he later explained to his sister Carol, "What I wanted was [a] wife in bed at night not somewhere having even higher adventures at so many thousand bucks the adventure." For her part, Marty wanted him to clean up his act: cut down the drinking, stop telling tall tales about the Crook Factory—and clean up his living quarters. But the writing was the main point of contention; Gregory Hemingway would remember his father's yelling at Marty, "I'll show you, you conceited bitch. They'll be reading my stuff long after the worms have finished with you."

True to form, he had another wife lined up before dispensing with the current one. He met Mary Welsh (Monks), a *Time* feature writer, in London, and quickly told her that he wanted to marry her. When she objected that they were both married to others, he allowed that the war might keep them apart for a while, but "just please remember I want to marry you."

Although journalists were not allowed to land with the troops, on D day, June 6, 1944, he was on a landing craft watching troops go ashore in France. Marty, however, had stowed away on a Red Cross hospital ship, and although she was not there on D day, she did "hit the beaches" on June 7, helping to evacuate the wounded. Hemingway never forgave her for her one-upsmanship. "Going to get me somebody who wants to stick around with me and let me be the writer of the family," he wrote to his son Patrick. By March of 1945 he and Marty had agreed to divorce. He divorced her in Cuba in December 1945; he and Mary, who had divorced her husband, Noel Monks, were married the following March.

## BACK TO NOVELS

Hemingway found it hard to begin writing again after the war. His next novel, *Across the River and into the Trees*, could have used Max Perkins's guiding hands (Perkins died in 1947); the critics lambasted it. He returned to one of the books he had set aside when he had written *Across the River*. *The Old Man and the Sea*, published in 1952, was a phenomenal success. *Life* magazine published the entire text, with an Albert Eisenstadt photograph of Hemingway on the cover, and sold 5,300,000 copies in two days. Even the critics proclaimed it a masterpiece. On May 4, 1953, he learned that it had been awarded the Pulitzer prize. The movie rights had been sold, and Spencer Tracy was to play the old man. Hemingway was back on top.

*Look* magazine offered to finance an African safari plus pay $10,000 for a 3,500-word story on the trip. Hemingway accepted, making another trip to Pamplona and a tour through Spain on his way to Africa. Once he was in Africa, this second safari became an adventure of an unintended kind: He and Mary survived not one but two plane crashes in two days. They arrived back in "civilization" (a town with medical facilities) to discover that their deaths had already been reported internationally.

When, in October 1954, Hemingway was told he had won the Nobel prize, he was ecstatic. But he wondered if his premature obituaries might have had as much to do with the award as *The Old Man and the Sea.*

## DECLINE

Revolution was brewing in Cuba; having seen it coming in Spain, Hemingway recognized the ominous signs. After some of President Batista's soldiers shot one of his dogs, he and Mary decided to return to the States for the fall and winter of 1958–59. He was there, in Idaho, when he heard that Fidel Castro had taken Havana. He pronounced himself "delighted," then modified it to "hopeful." But it still seemed a good time to buy a house in Idaho, and a good time to plan a trip to Spain for the following summer.

In Spain that summer of 1959, the year he turned sixty, he was greeted wherever he went as a celebrity. But he was drinking heavily; that, with the irregular hours and travel tensions, led to kidney problems. His moods were capricious and sometimes irrational.

Having accepted an offer from *Life* for an article on bullfighting, he returned to the Finca Vigía to write it. By July 1960 he had reluctantly concluded he would have to go back to Spain to get photographs and check facts. Four days after his sixty-first birthday, the Hemingways left Cuba for New York and then Spain, expecting to return that fall. Before they could return, the farmhouse and its contents—including Hemingway's collection of works by artists Juan Gris, Paul Klee, Georges Braque, and others, and several thousand books—had been appropriated by the Castro government.

Meanwhile, in Spain during August and September, Hemingway was suffering a breakdown. (Mary had stayed in New York.) Paranoid and delusional, he mistrusted friends as well as strangers. His friends managed to get him on a plane to New York, where Mary hoped that he was just suffering from overwork and would recover with rest. But he did not. Difficult family relationships, a family history of depression and a lifetime of alcohol abuse, at least five concussions and many other serious injuries over the years, diabetes, high blood pressure (treated with reserpine, which can cause depression)—it is impossible to assign his mental and emotional problems to any single cause, especially since he refused to consider any "talking" psychiatric therapy. By the end of the year, doctors at the Mayo Clinic had begun administering a series of electroshock therapy treatments. (Developed in Italy in 1938, the therapy, also known as electroconvulsive therapy, or ECT, had been found to help reduce the symptoms of patients suffering from major depression and delusional depression. There were also reports that it could cause memory deficits, which doctors believed were limited and temporary.)

The therapy seemed to help for a time, but his paranoia gradually returned. Worse, he was convinced that the shock treatments had destroyed his ability to write. Attempts at suicide were followed by more therapy, but there came a night when it all fell apart. He crept downstairs, retrieved from its locked cabinet a favorite shotgun, loaded it, and killed himself.

## CODA

In a November 1962 *Esquire* article called "The Big Bite," Norman Mailer examined the troubling question of how Hemingway could have committed suicide, which seemed the antithesis of all he believed in. He concluded:

> It is not likely that Hemingway was a brave man who sought danger for the sake of the sensations it provided him. What is more likely the truth of his own odyssey is that he struggled with his cowardice and against a secret lust to suicide all his life, that his inner landscape was a nightmare, and he spent his nights wrestling with the gods. It may even be that the final judgment on his work may come to the notion that what he failed to do was tragic, but what he accomplished was heroic, for it is possible that he carried a weight of anxiety with him which would have suffocated any man smaller than himself.

# CHAPTER 1

# The Hero
# and the Code

READINGS ON
ERNEST HEMINGWAY

# Hemingway's World

Robert Penn Warren

Hemingway's writing developed in method and in self-consciousness over the years, writes poet and author Robert Penn Warren. Yet Warren finds an underlying unity in the methods and motives through which Hemingway presented his world in all of his work. He writes of a violent world, whose heroes are men who live by a code of honor. This code, and the discipline needed to follow it, give meaning to life. The code helps Hemingway's heroes face "the great nada"—the nothingness of death.

It would be possible and even profitable to discuss *A Farewell to Arms* in isolation from Hemingway's other work. But Hemingway was a peculiarly personal writer, and for all the apparent objectivity and self-suppression in his method as a writer, his work forms a continuous whole to an uncommon degree. One part explains and interprets another part. It is true that there have been changes between early and late work, that there has been an increasing self-consciousness, that attitudes and methods that in the beginning were instinctive and simple have become calculated and elaborated. But the best way to understand one of his books is, nevertheless, to compare it with both earlier and later pieces and seek to discern motives and methods that underlie all of his work.

Perhaps the simplest way into the whole question is to consider what kind of world Hemingway wrote about. A writer may write about his special world merely because he happens to know that world, but he may also write about that special world because it best dramatizes for him the issues and questions that are his fundamental concerns—because, in other words, that special world has a kind of symbolic significance for him. There is often—if we discount mere literary fashion and imitation—an inner and necessary reason for the writer's choice of his characters and situations. What situations and characters did Hemingway write about?

They are usually violent. There is the hard-drinking and sexually promiscuous world of *The Sun Also Rises*; the chaotic and brutal world of war as in *A Farewell to Arms, For Whom the Bell Tolls*, many of the inserted sketches of *In Our Time*, the play *The Fifth Column*, and some of the stories; the world of sport, as in "Fifty Grand," "My Old Man," "The Undefeated," "The Snows of Kilimanjaro"; the world of crime as in "The Killers," "The Gambler, the Nun, and the Radio," and *To Have and Have Not*. Even when the situation of a story does not fall into one of these categories, it usually involves a desperate risk, and behind it is the shadow of ruin, physical or spiritual. As for the typical characters, they are usually tough men, experienced in the hard worlds they inhabit, and not obviously given to emotional display or sensitive shrinking, men like Rinaldi or Frederick Henry of *A Farewell to Arms*, Robert Jordan of *For Whom the Bell Tolls*, Harry Morgan of *To Have and Have Not*, the big-game hunter of "The Snows of Kilimanjaro," the old bullfighter of "The Undefeated," or the pugilist of "Fifty Grand." Or if the typical character is not of this seasoned order, he is a very young man, or boy, first entering the violent world and learning his first adjustment to it.

## A CODE THAT MAKES A MAN A MAN

The shadow of ruin is behind the typical Hemingway situation. The typical character faces defeat or death. But out of defeat or death the character usually manages to salvage something. And here we discover Hemingway's special interest in such situations and such characters. His heroes are not defeated except upon their own terms. They are not squealers, welchers, compromisers, or cowards, and when they confront defeat they realize that the stance they take, the stoic endurance, the stiff upper lip mean a kind of victory. If they are to be defeated they are defeated upon their own terms; some of them have even courted their defeat; and certainly they have maintained, even in the practical defeat, an ideal of themselves, some definition of how a man should behave, formulated or unformulated, by which they have lived. They represent some notion of a code, some notion of honor, that makes a man a man, and that distinguishes him from people who merely follow their random impulses and who are, by consequence, "messy."

In case after case, we can illustrate this "principle of sportsmanship," as critic Edmund Wilson has called it, at the center of a story or novel. Robert Jordan, in *For Whom the Bell Tolls*, is somehow happy as he lies, wounded, behind the machine gun that is to cover the escape of his friends and his sweetheart from [Francisco] Franco's Fascists. The old bull-fighter, in "The Undefeated," continues his incompetent fight even under the jeers and hoots of the crowd until the bull is dead and he himself is mortally hurt. Francis Macomber, the rich young sportsman who goes lion-hunting in "The Short, Happy Life of Francis Macomber," and who has funked it and bolted before a wounded lion, at last learns the lesson that the code of the hunter demands that he go into the bush after an animal he has wounded. Brett, the heroine of *The Sun Also Rises*, gives up Romero, the young bull-fighter with whom she is in love, because she knows she will ruin him, and her tight-lipped remark to Jake, the newspaper man who is the narrator of the novel, might almost serve as the motto of Hemingway's work: "You know it makes one feel rather good deciding not to be a bitch."

---

### A STYLE CARVED IN HARD WOOD

Ernest Hemingway is a great writer. Archibald MacLeish wrote of him:

Veteran out of the wars before he was twenty:
Famous at twenty-five; thirty a master
Whittled a style for his time from a walnut stick . . .

He used this hard style, carved in hard wood, to tell hard stories. Bloodied prize fighters, hired killers, disemboweled bullfighters, crippled soldiers, hunters of wild animals, deep-sea fishermen—Hemingway's favorite characters are men who deal in death and accept its risk.

André Maurois, "Ernest Hemingway," *La Revue de Paris*, March 1955.

---

It is the discipline of the code that makes man human, a sense of style or good form. This applies not only in isolated, dramatic cases such as those listed above, but is a more pervasive thing that can give meaning, partially at least, to the confusions of living. The discipline of the soldier, the form of the athlete, the gameness of the sportsman, the technique of an artist can give some sense of the human order, and can achieve a moral significance. And here we see how Hemingway's concern with war and sport crosses his concern with literary style. If a writer can get the kind of style at which Hemingway professes, in *Green Hills of Africa*, to aim, then "nothing else matters. It is more important than anything else he can do." It is more important because, ultimately, it is a moral achievement. . . .

But to return to the subject of Hemingway's world: the code and the discipline are important because they can give meaning to life that otherwise seems to have no meaning or justification. In other words, in a world without supernatural sanctions, in the God-abandoned world of modernity, man can realize an ideal meaning only in so far as he can define and maintain the code. The effort to define and maintain the code, however limited and imperfect it may be, is the characteristically human effort and provides the tragic or pitiful human story. . . .

## OBSESSED BY NADA

In one of the stories, "A Clean, Well-Lighted Place," we find the best description of the world that underlies Hemingway's world of violent action. In the early stages of the story we see an old man sitting late in a Spanish café. Two waiters are speaking of him:

> "Last week he tried to commit suicide," one waiter said.
> "Why?"
> "He was in despair."
> "What about?"
> "Nothing."
> "How do you know it was nothing?"
> "He has plenty of money."

The despair beyond plenty of money—or beyond all the other gifts of the world: its nature becomes a little clearer at the end of the story when the older of the two waiters is left alone, reluctant too to leave the clean, well-lighted place:

> Turning off the electric light he continued the conversation with himself. It is the light of course but it is necessary that the place be clean and pleasant. You do not want music. Certainly you do not want music. Nor can you stand before a bar with dignity although that is all that is provided for these hours. What did he fear? It was not fear or dread. It was a nothing that he knew too well. It was all a nothing and a man was nothing too. It was only that and light was all it needed and a certain cleanness and order. Some lived in it and never

felt it but he knew it all was nada y pues nada y nada y pues nada.* Our nada who art in nada, nada be thy name thy kingdom nada thy will be nada in nada as it is in nada. Give us this nada our daily nada and nada us our nada as we nada our nadas and nada us not into nada but deliver us from nada; pues nada. Hail nothing full of nothing, nothing is with thee. He smiled and stood before a bar with a shining steam pressure coffee machine.

"What's yours?" asked the barman.

"Nada."

At the end the old waiter is ready to go home:

Now, without thinking further, he would go home to his room. He would lie in bed and finally, with daylight, he would go to sleep. After all, he said to himself, it is probably only insomnia. Many must have it.

And the sleepless man—the man obsessed by death, by the meaninglessness of the world, by nothingness, by nada—is one of the recurring symbols in the work of Hemingway. In this phase Hemingway is a religious writer. The despair beyond plenty of money, the despair that makes a sleeplessness beyond insomnia, is the despair felt by a man who hungers for the sense of order and assurance that men seem to find in religious faith, but who cannot find grounds for his faith. . . .

The typical Hemingway hero is the man aware, or in the process of becoming aware, of nada. Death is the great nada. Therefore whatever code or creed the hero gets must, to be good, stick even in the face of death. It has to be good in the bull-ring or on the battlefield and not merely in the study or lecture room. In fact, Hemingway is anti-intellectual, and has a great contempt for any type of solution arrived at without the testings of immediate experience.

So aside from the question of a dramatic sense that would favor violence, and aside from the mere matter of personal temperament (for Hemingway describes himself on more than one occasion as obsessed by death), the presentation of violence is appropriate in his work because death is the great nada. In taking violent risks man confronts in dramatic terms the issue of nada that is implicit in all of Hemingway's world.

---

*nada y pues nada, etc.: nothing and after that nothing, etc.

# A Master Key to Understanding Hemingway

Philip Young

Hemingway's early stories show a boy who is wounded psychologically while growing up, and wounded again—physically as well as emotionally—as a young man, writes Philip Young, American literature professor and critic. Hurt in war, the hero is shell-shocked. It is important to note, says Young, that the hero is not only virile, he is also very sensitive. The Hemingway hero (who has much the same background from book to book, even when the names and situations change) never fully recovers from his wounds, although a second character—the "code hero"—often appears to show him how he could live properly and "conduct himself well in the losing battle that is life." The experiences of the Hemingway hero can be traced to the author's own youth. But the characters never really mature; their world does not lend itself to such mundane activities as filling out tax returns. The world of violence they inhabit may well be a prophecy of the world to come.

During his lifetime Ernest Hemingway was very probably America's most famous writer. His style, his "hero" (that is to say the protagonists of many of his works, who so resemble each other that we have come to speak of them in the singular), his manner and attitudes have been very widely recognized—not just in the English-speaking world but wherever books are widely read. It may be that no other novelist has had an equivalent influence on the prose of modern fiction, for where his work is known it has been used: imitated, reworked, or assimilated. In addition he had an extraordinary reputation as a colorful human being, and for over thirty years

From Philip Young, *Ernest Hemingway*, University of Minnesota Pamphlets on American Writers, no. 1 (Minneapolis: University of Minnesota Press, 1959), pp. 5-11, 44-45. Reprinted with permission from the publisher.

his every escapade was duly reported in the press. But for a long time neither he nor his work was well understood, and despite a considerable growth in understanding during the last decade, neither is yet understood as well as it might be.

There is never a simple key to any writer worth much attention, but in the case of Hemingway there is something that looks so like a key—even conceivably a master key—that it cannot escape any informed and thoughtful reader's notice. It lies waiting, curiously (a few might say fatefully), in the very first story in his first book of short stories, which was his first significant book of any kind.

The book appeared in 1925, and is called *In Our Time.* Very probably the author intended his title as a sardonic allusion to a well-known phrase from the Church of England's Book of Common Prayer: "Give peace in our time, O Lord." At any rate the most striking thing about the volume is that there is no peace at all in the stories. The next most striking thing about them (long unremarked, since it was not clear to readers that he was the central figure in the stories in which he appears) is that half of the stories are devoted to the spotty but careful development of a crucial but long-ignored character—a boy, then a young man—named Nick Adams. These stories are arranged in the chronological order of Nick's boyhood and early manhood, and are intimately related, one to another. Indeed in this aspect the book is almost a "novel," for some of the stories are incomprehensible if one does not see the point, and it is often subtle, of some earlier piece.

## THE EFFECT OF SHOCKING EVENTS

The most significant and interesting of these stories, however, is that first one. It is called "Indian Camp," and it reveals a great deal about what its author was up to for some thirty-five years of his writing career. It tells about a doctor, Nick's father, who delivers an Indian woman of a baby by Caesarean section, with a jackknife and without anesthesia. The woman's invalid husband lies in a bunk above his screaming wife; Nick, a young boy, holds a basin for his father; four men hold the mother down until the child is born. When it is over the doctor looks in the bunk above and discovers that the husband, who has listened to the screaming for two days, has cut his head nearly off with a razor.

A careful reading of this story will show that Hemingway is not primarily interested, here, in these shocking events: he is interested in their effect on the little boy who witnessed them. For the moment the events do not seem to *have* any great effect on the boy. But it is very important that he is later on a badly scarred and nervous young man, and here Hemingway is relating to us the first reason he gives why that is so.

The story has already provided, then, a striking insight into the nature of his work. But it has, in addition, a notable conclusion, as Nick and his father discuss death—and death specifically by one's own hand:

"Why did he kill himself, Daddy?"
"I don't know, Nick. He couldn't stand things, I guess."
"Do many men kill themselves, Daddy?"
"Not very many, Nick.". . .
They were seated in the boat, Nick in the stern, his father rowing. . . . In the early morning on the lake sitting in the stern of the boat with his father rowing, he felt quite sure that he would never die.

Now from a purely aesthetic point of view it is perfectly irrelevant, but from a human and biographical point of view perfectly unavoidable, to remark the uncanny fact that the originals of both these characters, making their first appearances here as doctor and son, were destined to destroy themselves. Clarence Edmonds Hemingway, M.D., the prototype for Dr. Adams, while in ill-health committed suicide with a pistol (a relic of the Civil War which the writer's mother later sent him) in 1928; the son, the prototype for Nick Adams, Ernest (Miller) Hemingway, blew most of his head off, with a favorite shotgun, in 1961. "He couldn't stand things, I guess."

As closely as this are many of the key events in the life of the hero tied to the life of the writer. Nearly as simple as this was his preoccupation with violence, and above all the fact of violent death. And seldom in the whole history of literature can there have been a more unlikely focusing on things-to-come as in this first little story.

The six following stories from *In Our Time* concerning Nick Adams are not so violent as "Indian Camp," but each of them is unpleasant or upsetting in some way or other. . . .

Immediately following "The Battler" comes a little sketch, less than a page long. . . . It tells us that Nick is in World War I, that he has been wounded, and that he has made a "separate peace" with the enemy—is not fighting for his country, or any other, any more. It would be quite impossible to exaggerate the importance of this short scene in any understanding of Hemingway and his work. It will be duplicated at more length by another protagonist, named Frederic Henry, in *A Farewell to Arms*, and it will serve as a climax in the lives of all of Hemingway's heroes, in one way or another, for at least the next quarter-century.

## SIGNIFICANT WOUNDS

The fact that Nick is seriously injured is significant in two important ways. First, the wound intensifies and epitomizes the wounds he has been getting as a boy growing up in the American Middle West. From here on the Hemingway hero will appear to us as a wounded man—wounded not only physically but, as soon becomes clear, psychologically as well. Second, the fact that Nick and his friend, also wounded, have made a "separate peace," are "Not patriots," marks the beginning of the long break with organized society as a whole that stays with Hemingway and his hero through several books to come, and into the late 1930's. Indeed the last story in this first volume, called "Big Two-Hearted River," is a kind of forecast of these things. It is obscure until one sees the point, and almost completely so; its author complained in 1950 that the tale was twenty-five years old and still had not been understood by anyone. But it is really a very simple "story." It is a study of a young man who has been hurt in the war, who is all by himself on a fishing trip, escaping everyone. He is suffering from what used to be called "shell shock"; he is trying desperately to keep from going out of his mind.

In his next two collections of short stories, *Men without Women* (1927) and *Winner Take Nothing* (1933), Hemingway included several more stories about Nick Adams. They do not change anything, but they fill in some of the gaps in his sketchy career. . . .

Further gaps in the picture we should have of Nick are filled by several stories Hemingway wrote in the first person. It is abundantly clear that the narrator of them is Nick, and in one of the tales, a war story called "Now I Lay Me," he is called by that name. This one is a story about insomnia, which Nick suffered for a long time following his wounding; he cannot sleep "for thinking," and several things that occupy his mind while he lies awake relate closely to scenes and events in stories already mentioned. "In Another Country" extends the range of Hemingway's essential interest from Nick to another individual casualty of the war, and thus points toward *The Sun Also Rises*, where a whole "lost generation" has been damaged in the same disaster. A further development occurs in "An Alpine Idyll," which returns us to a postwar skiing trip Nick took in a tale called "Cross Country Snow"; here the interest focuses on the responses of Nick and others to a particularly shocking situation, as it did in the more famous "Killers." But whereas in the earlier story Nick was so upset by the thought of the man who was passively waiting to be murdered that he wanted to get clean out of the town where the violence impended, healthy tissue is now growing over his wounds, and the point of the story lies in the development of his defenses.

## A NERVOUS HERO

By now it is perfectly clear what kind of boy, then man, this Adams is. He is certainly not the simple primitive he is often mistaken for. He is honest, virile, but—clearest of all—very sensitive. He is an outdoor male, and he has a lot of nerve, but he is also very nervous. It is important to understand this Nick, for soon, under other names in other books, he is going to be known half the world over as the "Hemingway hero": every single one of these men has had, or has had the exact equivalent of, Nick's childhood, adolescence, and young manhood. This man will die a thousand times before his death, and although he would learn how to live with some of his troubles, and how to overcome others, he would never completely recover from his wounds as long as Hemingway lived and recorded his adventures.

Now it is also clear that something was needed to bind these wounds, and there is in Hemingway a consistent character who performs that function. This figure is not Hemingway himself in disguise (which to some hard-to-measure extent the Hemingway hero was). Indeed he is to be sharply distinguished from the hero, for he comes to balance the hero's deficiencies, to correct his stance. We generally, though unfelicitously, call this man the "code hero"—this because he represents a code according to which the hero, if he could attain it, would be able to live properly in the world of violence, disorder, and misery to which he has been introduced and which he inhabits. The code hero, then, offers up and exemplifies certain principles of honor, courage, and endurance which in a life of tension and pain make a man a man, as we say, and enable him to conduct himself well in the losing battle that is life. He shows, in the author's famous phrase for it, "grace under pressure."

---

## THE BRUISER AND THE POET

One or two of the remarks Hemingway lets fall in [*A Moveable Feast*] throw a clear light on what he was doing [when he first began to write in Paris]. . . . The search was to discover a style, and he found, with the help of looking at Cézanne's pictures in the Musée du Luxembourg, that 'simple true sentences' were 'far from enough to make the stories have the dimensions that I was trying to put in them'. He was not then articulate enough to account for what he was doing and adds, besides 'it was a secret'. A secret that has escaped his many imitators; push the 'simple declarative sentence' as they will, the effect is utterly unlike Hemingway's; so elusive a secret that no one has ever parodied his style as devastatingly as he did, unconsciously. The secret lies in the complete and balanced fusion of the two distinct halves of his personality; of the man of action and the man of feeling, of the realist and the sentimentalist, of the bruiser and the poet. The attitude Hemingway turns to the world is designed like a tough plastic shield both to protect and reveal the essential innocence and sensibility of his nature.

Douglas Grant, *Purpose and Place: Essays on American Writers*, 1965.

---

This man also makes his first appearance in the short stories. He is Jack, the prizefighter of "Fifty Grand," who through a superhuman effort manages to lose the fight he has promised to lose. He is Manuel, "The Undefeated" bullfighter who, old and wounded, simply will not give up when he is beaten. He is Wilson, the British hunting guide of "The Short Happy Life of Francis Macomber," who teaches his employer the shooting standards that make him, for a brief period preceding his death, a happy man. And, to distinguish him most clearly from the Hemingway hero, he is Cayetano, the gambler of "The Gambler, the Nun and the Radio," who with two bullets in his stomach will not show a single sign of suffering, while the generic Nick, here called Mr. Frazer, is shamed to suffer less but visibly. The finest and best known of these code heroes appears, however, in Hemingway's most recent novel. He is old Santiago of *The Old Man and the Sea*. The chief point about him is that he behaves perfectly—honorably, with great courage and endurance—

while losing to the sharks the giant fish he has caught. This, to epitomize the message the code hero always brings, is life: you lose, of course; what counts is how you conduct yourself while you are being destroyed. . . .

## HEMINGWAY'S VIOLENT WORLD

It remains to say something about Hemingway's world—the world his experience caused his imagination to create in books. It is, of course, a very limited world that we are exposed to through him. It is, ultimately, a world at war—war either literally as armed and calculated conflict, or figuratively as marked everywhere with violence, potential or present, and a general hostility. The people of this world operate under such conditions—of apprehension, emergency, stiff-lipped fear, and pleasure seized in haste—as are imposed by war. Restricted grimly by the urgencies of war, their pleasures are limited pretty much to those the senses can communicate, and their morality is a harshly pragmatic affair; what's moral is what you feel good after. Related to this is the code, summarizing the virtues of the soldier, the ethic of wartime. The activities of escape go according to the rules of sport, which make up the code of the armistice, the temporary, peacetime modification of the rules of war.

Hemingway's world is one in which things do not grow and bear fruit, but explode, break, decompose, or are eaten away. It is saved from total misery by visions of endurance, competence, and courage, by what happiness the body can give when it is not in pain, by interludes of love that cannot outlast the furlough, by a pleasure in the countries one can visit, or fish and hunt in, and the cafés one can sit in, and by very little else. Hemingway's characters do not "mature" in the ordinary sense, do not become "adult." It is impossible to picture them in a family circle, going to the polls to vote, or making out their income tax returns. It is a very narrow world. It is a world seen through a crack in the wall by a man pinned down by gunfire. The vision is obsessed by violence, and insists that we honor a stubborn preoccupation with the profound significance of violence in our time.

We may argue the utter inadequacy of the world Hemingway refracted and re-created; indeed we should protest against it. It is not the world we wish to live in, and we usually believe that actually we do not live in it. But if we choose to look back over our time, what essential facts can we stack against the facts of violence, evil, and death? We remember countless "minor" wars, and two tremendous ones, and prepare for the day when we may be engaged in a holocaust beyond which we cannot see anything. We may argue against Hemingway's world, but we should not find it easy to prove that it is not the world we have been living in.

It is still too early to know which of all the worlds our writers offer will be the one we shall turn out to have lived in. It all depends on what happens and you never know at the time. "Peace in our time," however, was Hemingway's obscure and ironic prophecy, stated at the start and stuck to. From the beginning his eyes were focused on what may turn out decades hence to have been the main show. With all his obvious limitations, it is possible that he said many of the truest things of our age truly, and this is such stuff as immortalities are made on.

# Dealing with the Fear of Fear

## John Atkins

Much of Hemingway's work—as well as his life—has been an attempt to deal with the fear of fear, writes John Atkins, author of *The Art of Ernest Hemingway: His Work and Personality*. Hemingway had faced death when he was wounded in the First World War. The fear that he might falter when he faced death again drove him to place himself in danger to prove that he was not afraid. In his writing he continually explored the conjunction of fear and failure, and the hero's ability to succeed by overcoming the fear of fear.

The numbing sensation of fear is a central feature of Hemingway's work. Its expression rises quite naturally out of his war experience, but something congenital and deeper in his personality gives it especial significance. Many critics have approached this when referring to his competitiveness and his need to prove himself but I have never seen a full examination of the emotion-in-action.

First let us rid ourselves of the superficial view that the generation for which Hemingway spoke during the early part of his career was exceptionally subject to fear. This has been suggested by J. Donald Adams when he wrote, with that brand of self-satisfaction that professional reviewers assume as an outer skin, that 'we have already had our literary generation which surrendered to fears; it called itself the Lost Generation. Let us not have another.'[1]

Whether Mr. Adams likes it or not, we have had and will have others. Probably the best answer to him is contained in Wellington's statement that the man who says he is not afraid in battle is a damned liar, or some such phrase. The

1. *Literary Frontiers*

From John Atkins, *The Art of Ernest Hemingway: His Work and Personality* (London: Spring Books, 1952). Reprinted by permission of David Higham Associates, London.

generation that fought in the 1914–18 war (a much more horrifying experience than the last one) was badly scared. Perhaps a few escaped, but we are discussing normal, sensitive men. For some years the generation was branded and nothing they could do could hide it. But they grew out of the fear just as they managed to reorient themselves in other spheres of adaptation.

Everyone who knows Hemingway agrees that his wound in Italy marked him for life, spiritually as well as physically. The shock of this wound was so great that he has spent a large part of the rest of his life trying to assure himself that he is not scared. So far from luxuriating in his wound, as people like Adams imply, he has steeled himself to recover his normality. The discipline of his writing is perhaps a reflection of this other discipline in his mental life. When he was wounded he told a friend, 'I felt my soul or something coming right out of my body, like you'd pull a silk handkerchief out of a pocket by one corner. It flew around and then came back and went in again and I wasn't dead any more.' For a long time after that he was afraid to sleep in the dark. 'In the early years,' writes Malcolm Cowley, 'he forced himself to walk forward into danger because of his competitive spirit and because he was proving to himself that he was not that scared.'[2] (When camping, T.E. Lawrence used to sleep out in the rain just to satisfy himself that he could do it.)

Whenever Hemingway is writing of failure he usually ascribes it to fear. However it may be veiled it is the basic cause. A woman breaks from the embrace of an amorous matador and says, 'These are the hungry people. A failed bullfighter. With your ton-load of fear. If you have so much of that, use it in the ring.'[3] In the same story the dishwasher Enrique knows that he could never be a bullfighter because of his fear. He sculptures four perfect veronicas with his apron and finishes up with a rebolera [matadors' moves].

'Look at that', he said. 'And I wash dishes'.
'Why?'
'Fear', said Enrique. 'Miedo. The same fear you would have in a ring with a bull'.

The bullfighters know only too well that fear is their greatest enemy. Not the bull, but their own fear of the bull. Once fear creeps upon them they lose whatever is special to

2. 'Portrait of Mr. Papa'    3. 'The Capital of the World'

them. 'Bullfighters say that fear of a bull takes the type away from a bullfighter, that is, if he is arrogant and bossy, or easy and graceful, fear removes these characteristics.'[4] Once a man loses the thing that sets him apart, the thing that forms personality and creates individuality, he is lost. He sinks back into the herd and he will never excel in anything he puts his hand or mind to. Fear cannot be hidden, no matter how it decks itself; the bullfighter who was repulsed by the woman eventually lost her to a picador. His fear stood out and made him repulsive.

For some years Hemingway suffered this agony. He created Jake Barnes, his counterpart whose self-lack was entirely physical. But however hopeless Jake's predicament, it was certain. There was no turning back and there was no recovery. He knew exactly where he was and he could at least make the effort of adjustment. Hemingway's situation was different. Jake had nothing left to fear—he *was* impotent, he had no doubts on that score. Hemingway believed he had been face to face with death, in the vivid classical metaphor. He didn't know whether he dared face death again. Nor is it an easy matter to put it to the test. A man who fears sexual impotence can settle the question quite simply. A man who fears his own fear can put himself in danger but he can never be sure how he acquits himself. A certain degree of fear is normal and wholesome. How can a man know what this degree might be? Hemingway sought violence and brutality in an attempt to dissolve his doubts. While his legs healed he examined his mind anxiously. He found the bullring. This was a vicarious experience yet it was something not to turn away in horror or be sickened like so many Anglo-Saxons. It was a manner of dealing death, defying death and with it the fear of death.

But watching bullfights could not provide a complete exorcism. Not even by becoming one of the leading aficionados in Spain could he purge himself wholly. And so when he returned to Spain in 1937 he was still sick; 'he came with the apprehension of a man who has been hurt and twisted by the Great War and who was now voluntarily exposing himself to bombs and shells, afraid of being afraid once more and eager to share the experience of a people's struggle.'[5]

The Macomber story, probably his best known, has fear

---

4. *Death in the Afternoon*   5. Arturo Barea, 'Not Spain But Hemingway'

for its characteristic situation. Macomber has shown fear—
he has run away from a lion. The story concerns his attempt
to rehabilitate himself in the eyes of his wife and the white
hunter. From that moment onwards he must not only cease
to betray his fear but he must also show positive courage.
V.C.s[6] have told us that in the moment of courage they were
actually in a state of panic, and this is generally accepted.
But no such comforting rationalisation of the reality of
courage can satisfy the individual who has been discovered
in the act of cowardice. Hemingway's problem was a peculiar one. He had not been discovered in any act of cowardice
but he himself knew that he had been frightened. One part
of him accused the other and insisted on reparation.

### A WOUND THAT SCARRED HIS SOUL

In 1917 the United States entered World War I. Hemingway . . . found a way to leave for Europe as an ambulance
driver with the American Red Cross. Sent to the Italian
front, he soon found himself in the midst of bloody battles in
which he served with distinction. He was severely wounded
and decorated with the Italian *al Valore Militare* medal.

This wound left deep marks on him. He still bears its
actual scars along the entire length of one leg. And for a
time it scarred his soul as well. He was up in front of the
trenches at Fossalta di Piave, when fragments from an
Austrian trench mortar hit him. "I died then," he said. . . .

For a long time he could not forget that hell. He was in a
state of shock. He found it hard to fall asleep and, when he
did succeed, he would dream of that exploding trench mortar and awake with a start. [As he wrote in "Now I Lay Me":]

I myself did not want to sleep because I had been living for a
long time with the knowledge that if I ever shut my eyes in
the dark and let myself go, my soul would go out of my body.
I had been that way for a long time, ever since I had been
blown up at night and felt it go out of me and go off and then
come back. I tried never to think about it, but it had started to
go since, in the nights, just at the moment of going off to
sleep, and I could only stop it by a very great effort.

André Maurois, "Ernest Hemingway," *La Revue de Paris*, March 1955.

There is an insistence throughout this story that fear is
not to be condoned. Among the Christian virtues is courage

6. recipients of the Victoria Cross, a British military medal awarded for acts of remarkable valor

but fear is not rated as a sin. Indeed, the Christian is expected to show fear in certain situations, else he will be accused of pride. But Hemingway, Macomber and especially Mrs. Macomber are driven by a hard logic to regard fear as a sin that must be punished mercilessly. Macomber's fear was, of course, extreme and was expressed in an act of cowardice—yet cowardice is not a scientific term and in their hearts many people would sympathise with Macomber and regard his cowardice as justified. Not so his wife. After Wilson had killed the lion she

> had not looked at him nor he at her and he had sat by her in the back seat with Wilson sitting on the front seat. Once he had reached over and taken his wife's hand without looking at her and she had removed her hand from his. Looking across the steam to where the gunbearers were skinning out the lion he could see that she had been able to see the whole thing. While they sat there his wife had reached forward and put her hand on Wilson's shoulder. He turned and she had leaned forward over the low seat and kissed him on the mouth.

Macomber's fear deserved the bitterest humiliation.

The coward is a familiar character in Hemingway's work but he is never the traditional cringing coward. He is often a person who some of us would not call a coward at all. But the word or at least the thought springs readily to lips or mind. The dying man in 'The Snows of Kilimanjaro' is called a coward by his wife because he doesn't want to move. She is accusing him of accepting the end too tranquilly, she wants him to struggle. In *For Whom the Bell Tolls* we get a careful study of a confessed coward, Pablo. He is interesting because he admits his cowardice; it is quite clear how he has arrived at his condition, clear to himself and to us. But the epithet is not easily borne. The contempt for cowardice is so strong in our tradition we struggle against it even when we know it is a reality. When Pilar calls Pablo a coward he is offended.

> 'Coward', Pablo said bitterly. 'You treat a man as coward because he has a tactical sense. Because he can see the results of an idiocy in advance. It is not cowardly to know what is foolish'.
> 'Neither is it foolish to know what is cowardly', said Anselmo, unable to resist making the phrase.

Fear and its result in action, cowardice, being so common, attempts are always being made to interpret them as something else. Pablo denies the charge and had he been English might have said, 'Discretion is the better part of valour.' Or it can be dramatised, the shame buried in laughter, as in *The Good Soldier Schweik.* Today, when the language of heroism has become deflated, it is even fashionable to assert one's own cowardice, but there is an implicit agreement that this is a pose. We still have not reached the stage where fear, a spiritual wound, is viewed as tolerantly as a physical wound. Even the members of Pablo's partisan group, who realised that their leader's condition was something over which he had no more control than over a running nose, could not pardon him. They stated his malady accurately yet scornfully. 'In the first days of the movement and before too, he was something. Something serious. But now he is finished. The plug has been drawn and the wine has all run out of the skin.' A flesh wound heals, a broken limb mends. But fear feeds on itself and there is no surety of recovery. It follows a law resembling geometric progression. Once the original fear is planted a second fear branches, a fear that the first fear has become permanent. Then comes a third fear, that one's whole psyche has been poisoned.

One of the clearest accounts of how fear can disable a personality is to be found in this book. The partisans are discussing divination. For Robert Jordan the evil prognostications are always the product of fear.

'I believe that fear produces evil visions', Robert Jordan said. 'Seeing bad signs—'.

'Such as the airplanes today', Primitivo said.

'Such as thy arrival', Pablo said softly and Robert Jordan looked across the table at him, saw it was not a provocation but only an expressed thought, then went on. 'Seeing bad signs, one, with fear, imagines an end for himself and one thinks that imagining comes by divination', Robert Jordan concluded. 'I believe there is nothing more to it than that. I do not believe in ogres, nor soothsayers, nor in supernatural things'.

'But this one with the rare name saw his fate clearly', the gypsy said. 'And that was how it happened'.

'He did not see it', Robert Jordan said. 'He had a fear of such a possibility and it became an obsession. No one can tell me that he saw anything'.

It is probably safe to assume that everyone has his fears but they are restricted to particular fields and are therefore intermittent in their action. (The films are fond of this; many an actor has enjoyed portraying the sudden transformation of a fearless man into a knock-kneed coward at the sight of a lipstick-stained coffee cup or a nurse's apron.) The pit of fear is descended when a man's whole personality is warped, when he is nothing but fear on legs. Hemingway's best instance is Eddy, the rummy in *To Have and Have Not*, who can only approach normality by having his fear soaked out of him. 'I gave him a real one. I knew they wouldn't make him drunk now; not pouring them into all that fear.' (It is interesting to hear that a number of rummies figure among his close circle of friends; with a character like Hemingway in the vicinity it is probably worthwhile becoming a professional rummy. He will study them as closely as a psychoanalyst studies his pet Oedipus complex.) But drink is only effective for a very short time. 'It certainly was wonderful what a drink would do to him and how quick.' It didn't last long though.

The chief consolation is that fear can be overcome. All the multiplying fears can be destroyed by going to the root of the original one. Macomber discovered this when, after the lion episode, he steeled himself to face wild beasts again without shrinking. The fear fled from him as quickly as though it had been attacked by alcohol, but there was no need for it to return. It was not merely hiding. He could not conceal his elation at the defeat of his great enemy.

> Macomber's face was shining. 'You know, something did happen to me', he said. 'I feel absolutely different'.

To Wilson it was just as if Macomber was coming of age. He saw a fear that had perhaps only been brought out by the lion but probably much, much older now, being put to flight.

> Beggar had probably been afraid all his life. Don't know what started it. But over now. Hadn't had time to be afraid with the buff. That and being angry too. Motor car too. Motor cars make it familiar. Be a damn fire eater now. He'd seen it in the war work the same way. More of a change than any loss of virginity. Fear gone like an operation. Something else grew in its place. Main thing a man had. Made him into a man. Women knew it too. No bloody fear.

As for the genesis of fear, after which Wilson groped, only complete knowledge can reveal it. Even when we think we have traced it to a particular event, to an explosion in war or the face of a lion or some insignificant occurrence in the nursery, we may still be cheating ourselves. The event may be no more than the occasion on which a primal fear became objective. Fear may be in the human heritage. Like the waiter in 'A Clean, Well-Lighted Place,' we may be afraid of the void. Fear of the dark may be a memory of nothing. Fear of solitude may be fear of the thing we came from and, at least symbolically, return to. 'What did he fear? It was not fear or dread. It was a nothing that he knew too well. It was all a nothing and a man was nothing too. It was only that and light was all it needed and a certain cleanness and order. Some lived it and never felt it but he knew it was all nada y pues nada y nada y pues nada.'[7] How is this fear to be purged? If you are convinced that your whole existence is nada there is nothing you can do about it. It is like war.

Or the whole thing may be based on a vast, cosmic misunderstanding. We may be like the little boy patiently waiting to die because his temperature has soared impossibly far beyond forty-four degrees.

'About how long will it be before I die?'
'You aren't going to die. What's the matter with you?'
'Oh yes I am. I heard him say a hundred and two'.
'People don't die with a fever of one hundred and two. That's a silly way to talk'.
'I know they do. At school in France the boys told me you can't live with forty-four degrees. I've got a hundred and two'.
He had been waiting to die all day, ever since nine o'clock in the morning.
'You poor Schatz', I said. 'Poor old Schatz. It's like miles and kilometres. You aren't going to die. That's a different thermometer. On that thermometer thirty-seven is normal. On this kind it's ninety-eight'.[8]

We may be fooling ourselves all the time. Those who fear nothingness may be psychotic cases. Those who fear death may be using the wrong thermometer. Those who fear their own fear may still be romantic primitives. But the folly is no greater than the folly of envying another person his new car or having nothing better to do than lean out of the window and at this moment the world is in turmoil for that very reason—and a few others.

7. From *Winner Take Nothing*   8. 'A Day's Wait', from *Winner Take Nothing*

# The World Cannot Tolerate the True Individual

Joseph DeFalco

Hemingway's code demands that a man commit himself to an ideal, explains Joseph DeFalco, author of *The Hero in Hemingway's Short Stories*. A hero must not commit himself to the wrong ideal—but striving for the correct ideal often leads to death. This dilemma is illustrated in Hemingway's stories and nonfiction accounts of bullfighting, which present the sport as both a meaningful tragic ritual and an art that deals with death. Bullfighting offers a way to judge the morality of an individual: The true hero must reconcile himself to death and face death with dignity. Yet, by thus overcoming the sordidness of the world, the hero learns that he is no longer suited to live in that world.

Hemingway's clearest presentation of man's attempt to preserve an ideal is reflected in a group of stories called here, rather loosely, the Hemingway hero stories. Most of them examine the manifold difficulties encountered on the journey toward individuation, and a few examine the process in its totality. Here men face the ultimate test, or some symbolic reflection of that test, by trying to rise above the contingencies of life. Some of the stories point to a final, almost transcendental element in Hemingway's thought which at first glance seems at odds with his naturalistic technique.

In Hemingway's treatment of the ideals a man may hold, he forces consideration of the efficacy of the commitment to an ideal in a world where values have been prostituted to other gods, chiefly Mammon and unfaith. The man who commits himself to these false ideals is personified by Hemingway as "No-man." Those who adhere to the ideal of self-

From Joseph DeFalco, *The Hero in Hemingway's Short Stories* (Pittsburgh: University of Pittsburgh Press, 1963). Reprinted by permission of the author.

fulfillment are in the minority, and their very existence becomes intolerable to the majority who follow another course. The outcome of such a situation is always the same: persecution of those who hold the individual ideal. In most of Hemingway's stories he consistently champions the ideal of individuality. In those stories where other forces seem to emerge victorious, there is an underlying author sympathy which laments the fate of man in a world which can no longer accept a valid ideal. . . .

## THE BULLFIGHT RITUAL

Much has been written about the importance of the bullfight in Hemingway's fiction, and most of it is appropriate. An examination of Hemingway's direct declaration on the subject and a comparison with the implications of such stories as "Today is Friday" reveal that its centrality in Hemingway's thought goes far beyond the obvious. When seen as part of a general concept of a pastoral type of hero who is again and again crucified because of his ideals, such expressions reveal clearly that there is operative in Hemingway's fiction an ideal which at one level, at least, merges with the traditional Christian notion of crucifixion and redemption.

In many ways, Hemingway's nonfictional account of bullfighting, *Death in the Afternoon*, provides a touchstone for an understanding of the premises upon which much of the fiction rests. It soon becomes obvious in that work that the bullfight suggests a meaningful ritual activity for Hemingway, and his explanations point to his precise feelings on the subject. In spite of the many metaphorical allusions to bullfighting, his direct, contextual employment of the bullfight is to be found chiefly in one novel, *The Sun Also Rises*, and in two short stories, "The Undefeated" and "The Capital of the World." It otherwise appears in six of the "inter-chapters" of *In Our Time*, as well as in a number of nonfiction accounts.

Hemingway describes the bullfight as an "art." As such, it is capable of providing an aesthetic experience. Its nature is tragic: "The bullfight is not a sport in the Anglo-Saxon sense of the word, that is, it is not an equal contest or an attempt at an equal contest between a bull and a man. Rather it is a tragedy; the death of the bull, which is played, more or less well, by the bull and the man involved and in which there is danger for the man but certain death for the animal." The tragic nature of bullfighting is controlled by a rigidly disciplined ritual, and this has a threefold division, *los tres tercios de la lidia,* or the three thirds of combat.

Hemingway suggests that these "thirds" are analogous to the three acts in tragedy. The first, the *suerte de varas,* or trial of the lances, is the "act" of the capes, the picadores and the horses, and in it "the bull has the greatest opportunity to display his bravery or cowardice." The second "act" includes the planting of the *banderillas* in the bull's neck, "so that his attack will be slower, but surer and better directed." In the final "act" the matador prepares the bull for killing. Hemingway's own summary is necessary here for its bearing on the nuances of meaning he associates with the bullfight.

> These are the three acts in the tragedy of the bullfight, and it is the first one, the horse part, which indicates what the others will be and, in fact, makes the rest possible. It is in the first act that the bull comes out in full possession of all his faculties, confident, fast, vicious and conquering. All his victories are in the first act. At the end of the first act he has apparently won. He has cleared the ring of mounted men and is alone. In the second act he is baffled completely by an unarmed man and very cruelly punished by the banderillos so that his confidence and his blind general rage goes and he concentrates his hatred on an individual object. In the third act he is faced by only one man who must, alone, dominate him by a piece of cloth placed over a stick, and kill him from in front, going in over the bull's right horn to kill him with a sword thrust between the arch of his shoulder blades.

For Hemingway the bullfight carries the further possibility of some sort of aesthetic-cathartic response, and he directly articulates this: "I feel very fine while it is going on and have a feeling of life and death and immortality, and after it is over I feel very sad but very fine." All men do not have this capacity, of course, and in relation to those who view the bullfight it belongs only to a select few: "The aficionado, or lover of the bullfight, may be said, broadly, then, to be one who has this sense of tragedy and ritual of the fight."

With the ritual of the bullfight as the meaningful base, Hemingway actually constructs a hierarchy by which, in this special sense, the morality of an individual may be measured. It is not too distant from the gauge of the hero as he appears in the short stories in his quest for individuation. The "high priest" in this instance would be the matador himself, but only if he performs the functions of his office correctly and is the "complete bullfighter." The *aficionado* comes next, for he is the one who has the tragic sense and vicariously participates in the ritual at which the matador officiates. At the lowest end of the scale are those people who attend the bullfight and view the ritual performance but do not understand. These mere onlookers are the "tourists," the "well-fed, skull and bones-ed, porcellian-ed, beach-tanned, flannelled, panama-hatted, sport-shod."

The distinction among the levels of the hierarchy is related to the rest of the Hemingway canon, for an obvious value judgement based on an ideal is implied. Being a "complete bullfighter," the object of the ideal, may seem trivial at first glance, but when taken as a metaphor for a dominant attitude that persists through most of Hemingway's work, its importance gains magnitude. The appearance of an ideal other than stoicism has implications in relation to the traditional views of Hemingway's art. That is, idealism is not a framework in which Hemingway has often been thought to work.

## AN ART THAT DEALS WITH DEATH

Another important aspect of the bullfight as ritual concerns Hemingway's edict that as an art it deals with death. For Hemingway violent death is one of the simple and fundamental elements of life. Out of this view he derives a basic attitude that appears in many forms in his fiction: the only certainty in life is death. Atonement, with death as a certainty, formulates the ultimate task of many Hemingway heroes, and the motif in itself is a universal pattern. In the bullfight, as in other methods of seeking atonement, all efforts of the hero are directed toward reconciliation with the knowledge of death. Whether or not the rituals are effective is always determined more by the individual attributes of the hero than by external circumstance. Regardless of the particular situation, the Hemingway hero is always concerned with the problem of death. If he can become the equivalent of the "complete bullfighter," the possibility of atonement or eventual transcendence to some greater level of self-realization is ever-present. The type of hero that can accomplish such a feat is rare in any area of life, and the small likelihood of his ever appearing is related by Hemingway in connection with his discussion of the appearance of the "complete bullfighter": "But waiting for a messiah is a long business and you get many fake ones. There is no record in the Bible of the number of fake messiahs that came before Our Lord, but the history of the last ten years of bullfighting would record little else."

The recognition that death is inevitable is only one part of the ritual, for the *way* one faces death has equal importance. For Hemingway it is here that man records his true dignity or cowardice. The whole of the matter is not, however, simply that one understands that death will come and that he must prepare for it. On the contrary, the adjustment to death becomes a complex ritual in itself.

At the close of *Death in the Afternoon,* Hemingway relates that he took no formal notice of the "young phenomena" in the bullfight of the time. The reason for this inattention, he says, is that one cannot adequately judge a bullfighter until he has received his first serious wound. Similarly, in the fiction a hero can only prove his merit after he has been "wounded" in some fashion by the experiences of life. In much of Hemingway's fiction the wound is depicted as some physical hurt which either represents some deep inner hurt or foreshadows an emotional hurt. Accordingly the wound itself becomes just as much a certainty as death; indeed, the two are inextricably bound together. An identical situation exists in the bullfight, as Hemingway sees it, for it is a foregone conclusion that the matador will be gored if he continues to fight. The stroke is simply a matter of time, as is the case in the life experience, and the length of time depends upon the skill of the individual in avoiding the horns—either literally or metaphorically. Once a bullfighter has received a horn wound, if he lives and makes the proper adjustment he will be a better bullfighter and will approach the ideal. If he does not adjust to the certainty of the wound and to eventual death, he becomes a coward and does not truly participate in the ritual. . . .

In "The Capital of the World" Hemingway illustrates the extreme dangers for the man who would become the "complete bullfighter" and follow the ideal. The juxtaposition of the boy facing the knives of the mock-bull while the cowardly bullfighter makes advances to his sister provides a contrast and marks the differences between the two modes of adjustment. The boy as the uninitiated one exhibits characteristics that might have made him a "complete bullfighter," if he had lived. His early death signifies the almost impossible task that faces the man who would pursue the ideal. . . .

Defeat signifies surrender of the ideal, and the true hero in Hemingway's terms is the individual who never accepts the compromise. The end is always the same, however, for the world which Hemingway describes cannot tolerate the true individual for long. The victory for a hero is essentially the overcoming of the sordidness of the world in which he lives, and the knowledge such a success brings makes him unsuitable to live in that world.

# The Hero as a Good Sport

Delmore Schwartz

English professor and essayist Delmore Schwartz observes that Hemingway's characters are more often on holiday (frequently fishing, hunting, or skiing) or engaged in sports such as bullfighting than in earning a living. These intense and often solitary pursuits offer a better chance to display a character's individuality, mastery, and freedom. The holiday— often a sporting trip—allows the author to develop his theme of a sportsmanlike morality, a code that includes the proper manner of speech. Hemingway demonstrates proper (and improper) code behavior using an entire range of speaking styles.

When Hemingway was awarded the Nobel Prize last year [1954], *Time* magazine reported the honor under the rubric of *Heroes* instead of *Books*; and the summary of his career which followed spoke of Hemingway as "a globe-trotting expert on bullfights, booze, women, wars, big game hunting, deep sea fishing, and courage," adding that "his personality had made as deep an impression upon the public as his books." This excellent characterization may be misleading: it would be made more exact by asserting that the deep impression has been made upon the public by the personality encountered in Hemingway's books. This personality, which dominates all his writing, is a dramatized being combining the publicized public author with the typical heroes of his narratives.

The famous maxim, the style is the man, must become, to describe Hemingway's prose: the style is the personality. The leading characters in his novels are genuine and real but do not exist once and for all in the reader's mind as bywords and beings larger than life. The great characters of litera-

From Delmore Schwartz, "The Fiction of Ernest Hemingway," *Perspectives USA*, no. 13, 1955. Reprinted by permission of the Estate of Delmore Schwartz.

ture—Hamlet, Falstaff, Robinson Crusoe, Becky Sharp, Emma Bovary, Huck Finn, Leopold Bloom—possess that kind of reality; and it is the Hemingwayesque personality, more than his characters, which does also. This will be immediately recognized when Hemingway's narrative style is compared with his prose style when he writes in the first person, as in his books on bullfighting and big-game hunting. The style is exactly the same, whether it is fiction about an invented hero or the discourse of Hemingway himself, the most typical of his own heroes, when he speaks directly to the reader; it is not too much to say that he is then a heroic figment of his own narrative style, the robust, ebullient myth of a storyteller's imagination. It is because of this dramatized being that Hemingway has been the object of more publicity than any other American author, and the first to enjoy the kind of limelight accorded a Hollywood film star. For the majority of the reading public the distinction between the novelist and his books has become more and more a formality to be disregarded....

## A WRITER'S PRIMARY PATTERN

There is always a primary pattern at the heart of a serious writer's work, and it can be said that his style is the verbal realization of that pattern. It was the quality of Hemingway's style which attracted attention at the beginning of his career. It seemed the manifestation of a new point of view toward experience. His primary pattern can be seen in the clean, hard, bare, and clear-cut texture of the prose. The writing concentrates upon vivid sensation in the immediate present—and this is remarkable in a storyteller, since the art of fiction depends so much upon the present as arising from the past and moving toward the future. Perhaps Hemingway's human beings seek the immediacy and isolation of intense sensation because they have a profound need of being separate and alone, free of the past, history, the future, and hope, other human beings and all burdens.

In modern life, the experience of isolated enjoyment can be realized only under very special and privileged conditions. The most sensitive human beings feel a passionate devotion to sport because they find a fulfillment in it which they cannot attain in the serious pursuits by means of which they make a living.... Skiing and activities like it give the self a sense of intense individuality, mastery, and freedom.

In contrast, those activities which link the self with other human beings and are necessary to modern civilization not only fail to provide any such self-realization, but very often hinder it. The individual feels trapped in the identity assigned him by birth, social convention, economic necessity; he feels that this identity conceals his real self; and the sense that he is often only an anonymous part of the social mass makes him feel unreal. This is the reason that Hemingway's characters are so often drawn to the freedom of the holiday, are so often tourists, travelers, and expatriates, and so often appear at play and not at work. The desire for sensation is not the sensuality of the dilettante, but a striving for genuine individuality. The sensations of the immediate present have an authenticity which the senses make self-evident. Above all, those sensations which occur in the face of grave physical danger reveal the self's essential reality, since in the face of extreme threat, the self must depend wholly upon its own skill, strength, and courage.

Thus it is literally true that Hemingway's preoccupation with sensation is a preoccupation with genuine selfhood, moral character, and conduct. The holiday provides not only freedom, but good eating, good drinking, good landscapes, and good sexual intercourse under conditions which have the fairness of a game—so that drinking, making love, and most of the pursuits of the holiday become a trial of the self. Any concern with the self and its moral character requires a moral code, and the moral code in Hemingway is unmistakable. The rules of the code require honesty, sincerity, self-control, skill, and above all, personal courage. To be admirable is to play fairly and well; and to be a good loser when one has lost, acknowledging the victor and accepting defeat in silence. It is a sportsmanlike morality, which dictates a particular kind of carriage, good manners, and manner of speech: one must speak in clipped tones, condensing the most complex emotion into a few expletives or into the dignity of silence. . . .

## THE WHOLE RANGE OF STYLES OF SPEECH

Hemingway's style is the expression of the moral code at the heart of his writing. But it is neither primitive nor proletarian, as Mario Praz and Wyndham Lewis have suggested. It is sensitive to the whole range of difference between the speech of an aristocracy, the folk, the proletariat, the primitive, and the man in the street. Its devices include eloquent reticence, intensely emotional understatement, and above all the simplified speech which an American uses to a European ignorant of English. In fact what the American expatriate says and what he *hears* when he converses with a European are the very essence of Hemingway's style. The American, hearing the European speaking his own language, converts its idiom directly into a strange formalized English. When the Hemingway hero encounters the European, the dialogue which occurs intensifies the American hero's sense of his own attitudes and values to a remarkable degree, and results in a clear affirmation of Hemingway's moral code and his sense of the quality of modern life.

Hemingway's style is a poetic heightening of various forms of modern colloquial speech—among them, the idiom of the hardboiled reporter, the foreign correspondent, and the sportswriter. It is masculine speech. Its reticence, understatement, and toughness derive from the American masculine ideal, which has a long history going back to the pioneer on the frontier and including the strong silent man of the Hollywood Western. The intense sensitivity to the way in which a European speaks broken English, echoing his own language's idioms, may also derive from the speech of the immigrants as well, perhaps, as from the special relationship of America to Europe which the fiction of Henry James first portrayed fully.

In the story called *The Gambler, the Nun and the Radio*, there is an example of the complexity of Hemingway's style which is as adequate as one illustration can be. A wounded Mexican gambler is being questioned by an American detective who tells him that he is going to die and wants to know who shot him:

> "Listen," the detective said, "this isn't Chicago. You're not a gangster. You don't have to act like a moving picture. It's all right to tell who shot you. That's all right to do."

Although the Mexican understands English perfectly, this colloquial American speech must be translated into a stylized foreign version for him by Mr. Frazer, an American writer, who is also a hospital patient:

> "Listen, amigo," said Mr. Frazer. "The policeman says that we are not in Chicago. You are not a bandit and this has nothing to do with the cinema."
> "I believe him," said Cayetano softly. "*Ya lo creo.*"

"One can with honor denounce one's assailant. Everyone does it here, he says."

It must be noted, for the sake of emphasis, that *the moving picture* becomes *the cinema* and *that's all right* becomes *one can with honor*: these and other parallel expressions show how completely and precisely the style is a realization of the moral code and two entirely antithetical attitudes toward it.

# Cliquish Adolescents or Shattered Heroes in *The Sun Also Rises*

James Twitchell and Charles Child Walcutt

James Twitchell of Duke University and Charles Child Walcutt of Queens College of the City University of New York disagree on the depiction of the main characters of *The Sun Also Rises*. In Part I, Twitchell contends that Mike, Jake, and Bill are like a children's gang, with rigid standards of acceptance and a group slang that excludes outsiders. In Part II, Walcutt argues that they are not adolescents at all but damaged adults in a spiritually damaged world, just trying to hang on. In either case, they agree, Robert Cohn is an outsider.

## PART I

Alfred J. Levy has already amplified Frederick J. Hoffman's contention that *The Sun Also Rises* is plotted through a series of vignettes in which Jake Barnes encounters a cluster of characters involved in some symbolic action. Hoffman explains the importance of Jake's casual encounter with Wolsey and Crumb, and Levy interprets Jake's first meeting with Brett. But they say nothing of a third highly compressed scene in which Jake and Bill Groton meet and start to initiate the Englishman Harris into their "club." Although this initiation is ultimately unsuccessful and involves only a minor character, it details in microcosm the way Jake's society works to include new members. Conversely, it shows how and why people like Robert Cohn are kept out.

Mark Spilka has already pointed out how all the main characters, Mike, Jake, and Bill, are adolescents. Like children they feel safest when they are together in a gang. And like any gang they have rigid standards of acceptance. One

James Twitchell, "Hemingway's *The Sun Also Rises*," *Explicator*, December 1972. Charles Child Walcutt, "Hemingway's *The Sun Also Rises*," *Explicator*, April 1974. Reprinted with permission of the Helen Dwight Reid Educational Foundation. Published by Heldref Publications, 1319 18th St. NW, Washington, DC 20036-1802. Copyright ©1972, 1974.

of the most notable of these criteria is that they all talk in a certain way. Slang is very important, not just so that the "in" group can communicate, but also so that outsiders will be excluded. They talk to each other with "swells" and "grands" partly to identify themselves as being members, and partly to keep people like Robert Cohn out.

During the Burguete "Interlude" Jake and Bill have felt an almost childlike enthusiasm for the simple life of the outdoors. They have an almost religious feeling for the fresh life near the earth:

> Bill gestured with the drumstick in one hand and the bottle of wine in the other.
>
> "Let us rejoice in our blessings. Let us utilize the fowls of the air. Let us utilize the product of the vine. Will you utilize a little, brother?"
>
> "After you, brother."
>
> Bill took a long drink.
>
> "Utilize a little, brother," he handed me the bottle. "Let us not doubt, brother."

This word *utilize* that Bill happens upon comes to have a slang importance for both men. It becomes a kind of verbal "in" joke that reminds them that they both care deeply for many of the same things, and share the understanding that the world exists not just for them to appreciate but for them to "utilize."

In Chapter XIII, just after Harris is introduced to the Burguete scene, a telegram in Spanish arrives from Cohn that shows how hopelessly inept he is at using their language. Bill asks, "What does the word Cohn mean?" And Jake replies only: "What a lousy telegram." As opposed to Cohn, Harris immediately shows that not only does he like all the right things, good wine and fishing, but also that he speaks their language. He knows the password. Passing before a pub, Harris says, "Let's utilize it," and Jake comments that "he had taken up utilizing from Bill." Later, inside the club, Harris continues:

> "I say. You know this does utilize well."
>
> Bill slapped him on the back.
>
> "Good old Harris."
>
> "I say. You know my name isn't really Harris. It's Wilson-Harris. All one name. With a hyphen, you know."
>
> "Good old Wilson-Harris," Bill said. "We call you Harris because we're so fond of you."

As Harris becomes a member of the "club" he loses part of his surname as the group establishes a new identity for him.

Harris, like Cohn, is cut off from the rest of the world; like Cohn, he is alone and lonely. But unlike Cohn he "pays his own way." He insists on buying the wine, for, as he says, it gives him pleasure. And the confusion about his name may be a sign that like Cohn and the rest of the expatriates, he really doesn't know who he is. But that makes no difference to Jake and Bill, for he immediately becomes, like Count Mipplilopolous, "one of us."

This symbolic vignette ends with Harris' giving Jake and Bill a dozen flies he has tied himself. It is a touching gesture, reminiscent of the ways boys exchange parts of their hobbies as a token of comradeship. And just to make sure the point is not missed, Hemingway also has him give his card "with his address in London and his club." On the bus Jake and Bill converse:

> "Say, wasn't that Harris nice?" Bill said.
> "I think he really did have a good time."
> "Harris? You bet he did."
> "I wish he'd come into Pamplona."
> "He wanted to fish."
> "Yes. You couldn't tell how English would mix with each other, anyway."
> "I suppose not."

Their uncertainty about how Harris would have fitted into their club underscores their own peculiarly adolescent quality. When experience involves becoming close to people, they are remarkably unsure of themselves. What they forget is that it was Harris who refused their offer, not *vice versa.* They "suppose" that Harris might not mix well, partly as a way of not having to face the fact that Harris, lonely as he is, would rather fish than socialize. For in his own way he is a true *aficionado*, a passionate man.

## PART II

I must protest the treatment of Ernest Hemingway's *The Sun Also Rises* by James Twitchell, in which I think he makes a mistaken major assumption and thereupon a dubious deduction based on it. In the first place, Bill and Jake and the others are *anything* but adolescents. They are damaged people who, in a spiritually damaged world, are making heroic efforts to fend off that world and to maintain control of their precarious nerves. We have to understand both that they have been shattered by frightful experiences and that they see the world around them as exemplifying in its moral bankruptcy the forces that have shattered them. What organizes Hemingway's novel is the various ways that people respond, with their different selves, to this damaged world. Brett is desperate but fine. Bill isn't so damaged. Cohn is a phony. *He* thinks the others are having a ball. *He* thinks they are an admirable clique. But they are just trying to hold on. Jake is having the hardest time, and he tries hard to drink just enough and joke just enough and keep his nose clean enough so that he can hold Brett at bay, get some fundamental pleasures out of life, and not participate in the corruption. The winners are the Count, who knows the values, as he says (they are money, wine, food, courage, loyalty, friends—all basic, all gained because he has "paid" for them and because he has conscientiously given up the phony superficials that dazzle people like Cohn), and young Romero, who will achieve moments of highest grace in his tragic passage. In [poet Robinson] Jeffers' great image, Romero is the meteor to the Count's mountain ("Meteors are not needed less than mountains: Shine, perishing republic . . .").

This is the situation. It's not an adolescent club but an antiphony club; and here we come to that word "utilize." Solid people say "use." Phonies dress it up to "utilize," to absolutely no end but pretense. Jake and Bill horse around with "utilize" as a way of sharing their participation in the plight—and the defense—which they do not brag about openly.

CHAPTER 2

# Hemingway:
# The Man
# in His Work

READINGS ON
ERNEST HEMINGWAY

# Hemingway, Nihilism, and the American Dream

Samuel Shaw

In Hemingway's view, the human condition is essentially tragic, writes Samuel Shaw, author of the monograph *Ernest Hemingway.* Shaw says that the background for Hemingway's vision is nihilism—the denial of any objective basis for truth. Hemingway reflects the American form of nihilism, explains Shaw, which was more aggressive, naive, and adolescent than the European version. He loved life, although he felt it had no meaning; still, Shaw contends, he wanted to believe in something more. A deep compassion for humanity lies under the understated prose—a compassion that is often lost in the spare language and tough attitude of his writing.

In Hemingway's "The Snows of Kilimanjaro," Harry, the central character, is lying ill on an African plain. In the course of a hunting expedition a carelessly treated scratch on his knee has turned gangrenous. The infection has spread to his thigh; death is near. With the waiting buzzards as observers, Harry knows that he is dying. He has no patience with the efforts of his wife to reassure him:

> "You're not going to die."
> "Don't be silly. I'm dying now. Ask those bastards." He looked over to where the huge, filthy birds sat, their naked heads sunk in the hunched feathers. A fourth planed down, to run quick-legged and then waddle slowly toward the others.
> "They are around every camp. You never notice them. You can't die if you don't give up."
> "Where did you read that? You're such a bloody fool."

Hemingway saw himself and all humanity in Harry's situation—death sits with us from the beginning of life—and

like Harry he refused the solace of fine words, lofty sentiments, and spiritual clichés. When Harry asks where Helen
had read the old saw about not giving up, both Harry and
Hemingway are rejecting the genteel tradition in American
life, especially in literature, that had popularized and vul-
garized the American Dream. In nineteenth-century America people were hooked on spiritual hallucinogens. Hemingway would attempt to play it straight; he would try for the
truth. In his view, the human condition was essentially
tragic: defeat and frustration were built into the very structure of life. Popular literature and Sunday sermons might tell
Americans that hard-working people inevitably rose to af-
fluence, that bootblacks became millionaires and dedicated
their fortunes to the improvement of mankind, that all true
lovers finally were joined in everlasting marriage. For Hemingway, however, as he concluded in *Death in the Afternoon*,
"there is no remedy for anything in life."

## AMERICAN VS. EUROPEAN NIHILISM

The spirit of nihilism—the denial of any objective basis for
truth, especially moral truth—constitutes the background
for Hemingway's vision. In Europe, nihilism had been identified and analyzed in the nineteenth century by Nietzsche
and Dostoyevsky. Based as it was on the erosion of the classical and Christian foundations of Western civilization, the
nihilist position was essentially pessimistic. The depth of the
European cultural tradition, however, softened the harsh
outlines of nihilism. Nietzsche ends in an ecstatic affirmation of life; Dostoyevsky, in a plea for an existential leap into
religious belief. Both men found their way back to the tradition after cutting away its rational underpinning.

When the nihilist spirit reached America in the twentieth
century it assumed a truculence that was a reaction to the
gentility of nineteenth-century American culture. One
thinks of Robert Ingersoll challenging God to strike him
dead. There is something naive and daringly adolescent in
the American form of nihilist thought. In Europe nineteenth-
century writing had prepared the way for the shock of Nietzsche. Novelists like Balzac and Flaubert had analyzed in
depth the shortcomings of bourgeois society. In America, the
optimism of an Emerson or a Whitman offered no effective
cushion for the shock. Writers like Hawthorne and Melville,
who saw the darker side of the American experience, still

expressed their vision in genteel prose. It was writing in the spirit of Sunday rather than of workaday Monday. Mark Twain, in retrospect, came to grips with the realities of American life, but in his own time he was accepted only as a humorist and entertainer.

---

#### COURAGE WAS THE ONLY VIRTUE

If death was all—searing and sudden or prolonged with humiliation—then courage was the only virtue. The courage of the bullfighter, no more useless than all other courage, was a self-sufficient value, daring and inflicting with grave and serene style the annihilation of death.

Edgar Johnson, "Farewell the Separate Peace: The Rejections of Ernest Hemingway," *Sewanee Review*, July–September 1940.

---

Hemingway reflects a stark, often rhetorical nihilism with some of the angry tones of midwestern populism. In America, after the disillusionment with the war to save the world for democracy [World War I], it was impossible to use the old foundations to justify the popular philosophic and moral verities. The underside of American life was exposed for examination. The muckrakers—Lincoln Steffens, Ida Tarbell, and Samuel Hopkins Adams, among others—had begun even earlier to expose the seamy side of American economic and social life. In fiction William Dean Howells, Theodore Dreiser, and Upton Sinclair had already presented American life with some of the rosiness filtered out. Dreiser's Sister Carrie does not suffer the torments of conscience when she becomes a "fallen" woman, nor does she inevitably slide into the life of a prostitute. In the cities of America, survival was enough of a problem to make irrelevant the moral clichés of the past.

After Charles Lyell, Darwin, Marx, and Freud, the easy answers are gone. Dostoyevsky's Ivan Karamazov knows what has happened to the world when he observes that if God is dead, everything is permitted. If life and death have no transcendent significance, if man is made in the image of an ape, how do we determine what is moral and what immoral?

Hemingway does not approach the problem as a philosopher. If he reflects the spirit of nihilism, it is because he breathed the air of America. The malaise was there, the sudden awareness of Adam after he ate the apple. One did not need to pick it up in a college lecture hall. Hemingway, whose formal education never went beyond high school, remained antiacademic and antiintellectual all his life. He always preferred the thing to the theory. His origins are closer to American experience than to literary reflections of that experience.

## A REJECTION OF AMERICAN IDEALISM

The recognition of nothingness, *nada*—the loss of ultimate meaning in life—is Hemingway's starting point. In *A Farewell to Arms*, Frederic Henry, a volunteer ambulance driver in the World War I Italian army, expressed uneasiness before high-sounding phrases that cannot be believed in:

> I was always embarrassed by the words sacred, glorious, and sacrifice and the expression in vain. We had heard them, sometimes standing in the rain almost out of earshot, so that only the shouted words came through, and had read them, on proclamations that were slapped up by billposters over other proclamations, now for a long time, and I had seen nothing sacred, and the things that were glorious had no glory and the sacrifices were like the stockyards at Chicago if nothing was done with meat except to bury it. There were many words that you could not stand to hear and finally only the names of places had dignity.

... Hemingway was clearly in violent reaction to nineteenth-century American idealism. The optimism of an Emerson or a Whitman made him blush. The life Hemingway saw was brutal and degrading.

How to live then? What to do with one's life? For one thing, Hemingway did not reject life itself; a man may enjoy experience even if he can find no firm philosophic anchor. By temperament he was a man who appreciated the good things of life. There were spectacles to be enjoyed, whiskey to be drunk, women to be loved. There were forests to be camped in, streams with trout to be caught, snow on the mountains, pure air to breathe, and cool dry nights when sleep comes easy. As the existentialist Ivan Karamazov said it, one may love life more than the meaning of life.

Love of life in Hemingway, however, is accompanied by an acute awareness of *nada.* The smell of death suffuses his writing. Hemingway's obsession with death is expressed in most of his works. In several instances, his anguish overflows into the artistic creation and results in a personal confession....

By his own admission, Hemingway wrote about what he had actually experienced. Most of his fiction is obviously close to the events of his life. It is a mistake, however, to view Hemingway's fiction as autobiography. One must always keep a distance between the work of art and the artist's life, although that distance is infinitely varied and infinitely complex. In a sense, a writer appears in all his fictional characters and in none. One may read "The Snows of Kilimanjaro" as a confessional story and go very wide of the mark.

Artistic truth clearly is concerned with life truth, but that is about all one can safely say. Hemingway's "truth" was not a mere transcript of his life. In his introduction to *Men at War*, a collection, edited by him, of great battle scenes from European and American literature, Hemingway declared that "a writer's job is to tell the truth," and that his imagination, based on his own experience, "should produce a truer account than anything factual can be." In his aesthetics Hemingway was close to Aristotle's concept of the probable. His aim was universal truth.

## THERE IS MORE TO HEMINGWAY THAN THE CODE HERO

The first requirement for the Hemingway hero is freedom from illusions. He must know the score on life and death, and he must not discuss that score openly. He must be stoic in the losing battle; he must not be afraid. From this position Hemingway developed an approved code of behavior. One does not make a fuss about things or behave clumsily, one drinks heavily but does not get drunk, one loves but does not seek possession. The big-game hunter, the athlete, the good soldier, especially the bullfighter, became for Hemingway ideal representations of the man who lives with death but does not overdramatize himself. He has guts, which Hemingway defined as "grace under pressure." It is this code that leaves Hemingway open to caricature—the code hero as a combination of Tarzan and Wild Bill Hickok with headquarters at Club 21.

There is more in Hemingway, however. His nihilism, which may even have included an element of posturing, was always at war with his compassion and romanticism. His heart sought and *wanted* to believe in something more, something that made the game worth playing. He finally came to an essentially tragic affirmation of life, as affirmative and tragic as contemporary Americans are apparently capable of accepting. Hemingway is the prototype of the naysayer who, one suspects, loves his fellowmen, even his country, more than he will allow himself to express. When he says something good about humanity he finds it necessary to conclude with something like "and all that sort of jazz.". . .

Hemingway, shorn of illusions, still had to grapple with the problem of morality. In *Death in the Afternoon* he said that "what is moral is what you feel good after and what is immoral is what you feel bad after." This quotation has often been cited as proof of Hemingway's nihilism and hedonism. It sounds tough and honest in its simplicity, but one must ask the inevitable question—how long after? Hemingway surely appreciated immediate physical pleasure, but he did not stop with it. He upheld political, moral, and spiritual values requiring self-sacrifice and commitment to high ideals. In his last books Hemingway came close to affirming transcendental values and an asceticism of sorts.

Even in Hemingway's earliest successful novel, *The Sun Also Rises*, the promiscuous Brett Ashley gives up Pedro Romero, her matador lover, because she feels that she is not good for him. She tells Jake, whose love for her has been made impossible of fulfillment by his emasculation through a war wound, that "It makes one feel rather good deciding not to be a bitch. . . . It's sort of what we have instead of God." Hemingway's tough moral measure is closer to the idea of the Christian conscience and the inner check than one would first think. In this respect he is very much like Henry James, one of his favorite novelists.

Byron's Don Juan said that he laughed at mortal things to keep himself from weeping; Hemingway understates so that he will not weep. His characters feel more deeply than they are willing to say or Hemingway to make explicit. Hemingway's embarrassment with "fine" language, and his unwillingness to expatiate on spiritual states, are literary manifestations of the modern rejection of didacticism and sentimentality. Underneath the firm, muscular prose, however, is a deep compassion for the human condition. The Hemingway style is much tougher than the message conveyed by it.

It is this spare language and this tough attitude that have been widely imitated, sometimes to the point of parody. Little Caesar (W.R. Burnett's gangster) and Sam Spade (Dashiell Hammett's private detective) are Hemingway's illegitimate offspring.

In Hemingway's best work, especially in the successful short stories, the taut, uncluttered language forces the reader to supply the emotional concomitant. Hemingway was completely aware of what he was doing. In *Death in the Afternoon* he explains his method:

> If a writer of prose knows enough about what he is writing about he may omit things that he knows and the reader, if the writer is writing truly enough, will have a feeling of those things as strongly as though the writer had stated them. The dignity of movement of an iceberg is due to only one-eighth of it being above water.

It has been said repeatedly that Hemingway's style is his greatest achievement. If achievement is measured mainly by influence on other writers, that judgment is correct. The stature of a writer in the long run, however, is determined in equal measure by what he said about his own time, and by its continuing applicability to all time. In short, the critical emphasis on Hemingway as stylist does not do justice to him. He has not been given credit for bringing to fiction a new dimension, some new correspondence with the indefinable *reality* that creative literature strives to fathom. In some way he has brought literature closer to life. If he offers no apocalyptic vision, he still leaves us with the feeling that this is the way things really are.

# Elaborating a Personal Myth

Ralph Ellison

Hemingway's sense of rugged individualism, especially as expressed in his early work, signals a loss
of humanism in American culture, according to
Ralph Ellison, essayist and author of *Invisible Man*.
In this 1946 essay, Ellison maintains that earlier authors such as Mark Twain dealt with personal responsibility and the conflicting drives toward humanism and individualism. By now, he contends,
individualism has "won" in American culture, and
the sense of responsibility in literature has given
way to a simpler desire for technical perfection in
writing. Hemingway, like other writers of his time,
abandoned the national democratic myth, the dream
of a single ethic for all men based on the Constitution and the Declaration of Independence. This degrading of a great social myth, says Ellison, conditions readers to lower social values and a decreased
sense of responsibility.

Huck Finn's acceptance of the evil implicit in his "emancipation" of Jim [in *The Adventures of Huckleberry Finn*] represents Mark Twain's acceptance of his personal responsibility in the condition of society. This was the tragic face
behind his comic mask.

But by the twentieth century this attitude of tragic responsibility had disappeared from our literature along with
that broad conception of democracy which vitalized the
work of our greatest writers. After Twain's compelling
image of black and white fraternity the Negro generally dis-
appears from fiction as a rounded human being. And if already in Twain's time a novel which was optimistic concerning a democracy which would include all men could

From Ralph Ellison, "Twentieth-Century Fiction and the Black Mask of Humanity,"
*Confluence*, 1953. Copyright ©1953 by the President and Fellows of Harvard College.
(Originally written in 1946; unpublished until 1953.)

not escape being banned from public libraries, by our day his great drama of interracial fraternity had become, for most Americans at least, an amusing boy's story and nothing more. But . . . Huck's relationship to Jim, the river, and all they symbolize, is that of a humanist; in his relation to the community he is an individualist. He embodies the two major conflicting drives operating in nineteenth-century America. And if humanism is man's basic attitude toward a social order which he accepts, and individualism his basic attitude toward one he rejects, one might say that Twain, by allowing these two attitudes to argue dialectically in his work of art, was as highly moral an artist as he was a believer in democracy, and vice versa.

## HEMINGWAY MISSED THE POINT

History, however, was to bring an ironic reversal to the direction which Huckleberry Finn chose, and by our day the divided ethic of the community had won out. In contrast with Twain's humanism, individualism was thought to be the only tenable attitude for the artist.

Thus we come to Ernest Hemingway, one of the two writers whose art is based most solidly upon Mark Twain's language, and one who perhaps has done most to extend Twain's technical influence upon our fiction. It was Hemingway who pointed out that all modern American writing springs from *Huckleberry Finn.* (One might add here that equally as much of it derives from Hemingway himself.) But by the twenties the element of rejection implicit in Twain had become so dominant an attitude of the American writer that Hemingway goes on to warn us to "stop where the Nigger Jim is stolen from the boys. That is the real end. The rest is just cheating."

So thoroughly had the Negro, both as man and as a symbol of man, been pushed into the underground of the American conscience that Hemingway missed completely the structural, symbolic and moral necessity for that part of the plot in which the boys rescue Jim. Yet it is precisely this part which gives the novel its significance. Without it, except as a boy's tale, the novel is meaningless. Yet Hemingway, a great artist in his own right, speaks as a victim of that culture of which he is himself so critical, for by his time that growing rift in the ethical fabric pointed out by Twain had become completely sundered—snagged upon the irrepressible moral reality of the Negro. Instead of the single democratic ethic for every man, there now existed two: one, the idealized ethic of the Constitution and the Declaration of Independence, reserved for white men; and the other, the pragmatic ethic designed for Negroes and other minorities, which took the form of discrimination. Twain had dramatized the conflict leading to this division in its earlier historical form, but what was new here was that such a moral division, always a threat to the sensitive man, was ignored by the artist in the most general terms, as when Hemingway rails against the rhetoric of the First World War.

## USING AFRICANISM AS A FICTIONAL TECHNIQUE

Race has become metaphorical—a way of referring to and disguising forces, events, classes, and expressions of social decay and economic division far more threatening to the body politic than biological "race" ever was. . . . I remain convinced that the metaphorical and metaphysical uses of race occupy definitive places in American literature, in the "national" character, and ought to be a major concern of the literary scholarship that tries to know it. . . .

Hemingway's work could be described as innocent of nineteenth-century ideological agenda as well as free of what may be called recent, postmodernist sensitivity. With this in mind, . . . look at how Hemingway's fiction is affected by an Africanist presence. . . .

[In *To Have and Have Not*] we see Africanism used as a fundamental fictional technique by which to establish character. Within a milieu that threatens the dissolution of all distinctions of value—the milieu of the working poor, the unemployed, sinister Chinese, terrorist Cubans, violent but cowardly blacks, upper-class castrati, female predators— Harry and Marie (an ex-prostitute) gain potency, a generative sexuality. They solicit our admiration by the comparison that is struck between their claims to fully embodied humanity and a discredited Africanism. The voice of the text is complicit in these formulations: Africanism becomes not only a means of displaying authority but, in fact, constitutes its source.

Toni Morrison, *Playing in the Dark: Whiteness and the Literary Imagination.* New York: Vintage, 1992.

Hemingway's blindness to the moral values of *Huckleberry Finn* despite his sensitivity to its technical aspects duplicated the one-sided vision of the twenties. Where Twain, seeking for what Melville called "the common continent of man," drew upon the rich folklore of the frontier (not omitting the Negro's) in order to "Americanize" his idiom, thus broadening his stylistic appeal, Hemingway was alert only to Twain's technical discoveries—the flexible colloquial language, the sharp naturalism, the thematic potentialities of adolescence. Thus what for Twain was a means to a moral end became for Hemingway an end in itself. And just as the trend toward technique for the sake of technique and production for the sake of the market lead to the neglect of the human need out of which they spring, so do they lead in literature to a marvelous technical virtuosity won at the expense of a gross insensitivity to fraternal values.

It is not accidental that the disappearance of the human Negro from our fiction coincides with the disappearance of deep-probing doubt and a sense of evil. Not that doubt in some form was not always present, as the works of the lost generation, the muckrakers and the proletarian writers make very clear. But it is a shallow doubt, which seldom turns inward upon the writer's own values; almost always it focuses outward, upon some scapegoat with which he is seldom able to identify himself as Huck Finn identified himself with the scoundrels who stole Jim and with Jim himself. This particular naturalism explored everything except the nature of man.

And when the artist would no longer conjure with the major moral problem in American life, he was defeated as a manipulator of profound social passions. . . . And now the tradition of avoiding the moral struggle had led not only to the artistic segregation of the Negro but to the segregation of real fraternal, i.e., democratic, values.

The hard-boiled school represented by Hemingway, for instance, is usually spoken of as a product of World War I disillusionment, yet it was as much the product of a tradition which arose even before the Civil War—that tradition of intellectual evasion for which Thoreau criticized Emerson in regard to the Fugitive Slave Law, and which had been growing swiftly since the failure of the ideals in whose name the Civil War was fought. . . .

## TECHNICAL PERFECTION, NOT MORAL INSIGHT

It is instructive that Hemingway, born into a civilization characterized by violence, should seize upon the ritualized

violence of the culturally distant Spanish bullfight as a lab-
oratory for developing his style. For it was, for Americans, an
amoral violence (though not for the Spaniards) which he
was seeking. Otherwise he might have studied that ritual of
violence closer to home, that ritual in which the sacrifice is
that of a human scapegoat, the lynching bee. Certainly this
rite is not confined to the rope as agency, nor to the South as
scene, nor even to the Negro as victim.

But let us not confuse the conscious goals of twentieth-
century fiction with those of the nineteenth century, let us
take it on its own terms. Artists such as Hemingway were
seeking a technical perfection rather than moral insight. (Or
should we say that theirs was a morality of technique?) They
desired a style stripped of unessentials, one that would appeal without resorting to what was considered worn-out
rhetoric, or best of all without any rhetoric whatsoever. It
was felt that through the default of the powers that ruled society the artist had as his major task the "pictorial presentation of the evolution of a personal problem." Instead of
recreating and extending the national myth as he did this,
the writer now restricted himself to elaborating his personal
myth. And although naturalist in his general style, he was
not interested, like Balzac, in depicting a society, or even,
like Mark Twain, in portraying the moral situation of a na-
tion. Rather he was engaged in working out a personal problem through the evocative, emotion-charged images and rit-
ual-therapy available through the manipulation of art forms.
And while art was still an instrument of freedom, it was now
mainly the instrument of a questionable personal freedom
for the artist, which too often served to enforce the "unfree-
dom" of the reader.

This because it is not within the province of the artist to
determine whether his work is social or not. Art by its nature
*is* social. And while the artist can determine within a certain
narrow scope the type of social effect he wishes his art to
create, here his will is definitely limited. Once introduced
into society, the work of art begins to pulsate with those
meanings, emotions, ideas brought to it by its audience and
over which the artist has but limited control. The irony of
the "lost generation" writers is that while disavowing a social role it was the fate of their works to perform a social
function which re-enforced those very social values which
they most violently opposed. How could this be? Because in

its genesis the work of art, like the stereotype, is personal; psychologically it represents the socialization of some profoundly personal problem involving guilt (often symbolic murder—parricide, fratricide—incest, homosexuality, all problems at the base of personality) from which by expressing them along with other elements (images, memories, emotions, ideas) he seeks transcendence. To be effective as personal fulfillment, if it is to be more than dream, the work of art must simultaneously evoke images of reality and give them formal organization. And it must, since the individual's emotions are formed in society, shape them into socially meaningful patterns (even Surrealism and Dadaism depended upon their initiates). Nor, as we can see by comparing literature with reportage, is this all. The work of literature differs basically from reportage not merely in its presentation of a pattern of events, nor in its concern with emotion (for a report might well be an account of highly emotional events), but in the deep personal necessity which cries full-throated in the work of art and which seeks transcendence in the form of ritual.

## THE RITE OF PERSONAL EXPIATION

Malcolm Cowley, on the basis of the rites which he believes to be the secret dynamic of Hemingway's work, has identified him with Poe, Hawthorne and Melville, "the haunted and nocturnal writers," he calls them, "the men who dealt with images that were symbols of an inner world." In Hemingway's work, he writes, "we can recognize rites of animal sacrifice . . . of sexual union . . . of conversion . . . and of symbolic death and rebirth." I do not believe, however, that the presence of these rites in writers like Hemingway is as important as the fact that here, beneath the dead-pan prose, the cadences of understatement, the anti-intellectualism, the concern with every "fundamental" of man except that which distinguishes him from the animal—that here is the twentieth-century form of that magical rite which during periods of great art has been to a large extent public and explicit. Here is the literary form by which the personal guilt of the pulverized individual of our rugged era is expiated: not through his identification with the guilty acts of an Oedipus, a Macbeth or a Medea, by suffering their agony and loading his sins upon their "strong and passionate shoulders," but by being gored with a bull, hooked with a fish, impaled with a grasshopper on a fishhook; not by identifying himself with human heroes, but with those who are indeed defeated.

On the social level this writing performs a function similar to that of the stereotype: it conditions the reader to accept the less worthy values of society, and it serves to justify and absolve our sins of social irresponsibility. With unconscious irony it advises stoic acceptance of those conditions of life which it so accurately describes and which it pretends to reject. And when I read the early Hemingway I seem to be in the presence of Huckleberry Finn who, instead of identifying himself with humanity and attempting to steal Jim free, chose to write the letter which sent him back into slavery. So that now he is a Huck full of regret and nostalgia, suffering a sense of guilt that fills even his noondays with nightmares, and against which, like a terrified child avoiding the cracks in the sidewalk, he seeks protection through the compulsive minor rituals of his prose.

The major difference between nineteenth- and twentieth-century writers is not in the latter's lack of personal rituals—a property of all fiction worthy of being termed literature—but in the social effect aroused within their respective readers. Melville's ritual (and his rhetoric) was based upon materials that were more easily available, say, than Hemingway's. They represented a blending of his personal myth with universal myths as traditional as any used by Shakespeare or the Bible, while until *For Whom the Bell Tolls* Hemingway's was weighted on the personal side. The difference in terms of perspective of belief is that Melville's belief could still find a public object. Whatever else his works were "about" they also managed to be about democracy. But by our day the democratic dream had become too shaky a structure to support the furious pressures of the artist's doubt. And as always when the belief which nurtures a great social myth declines, large sections of society become prey to superstition. For man without myth is Othello with Desdemona gone: chaos descends, faith vanishes and superstitions prowl in the mind.

# Rejecting "A Separate Peace"

Edgar Johnson

Because Hemingway often portrays unsophisticated and even ignorant people, many critics believe he himself is simple-minded. But writer Edgar Johnson notes that he is, in fact, an intellectual, whose body of work shows significant evidence of intellectual growth. In *To Have and Have Not*, Hemingway begins to reject his earlier idea that the hero must stand alone in the world. As his hero is dying, he understands that "a separate peace" makes defeat inevitable.

Few modern writers reveal a more consistent intellectual development than Ernest Hemingway. In both his themes and the meaning he has found in them he has moved steadily and even logically from the earliest work of *In Our Time* to the significant orientation of *The Fifth Column*. The logic of this development has for the most part remained unnoticed by critics who have failed to realize that Hemingway, far from being a child of nature, is in fact an intellectual. They have presented him, consequently, as a sort of savage endowed with style, gifted but brainless, and the angry darts of *The Sun Also Rises* as those of an *enfant terrible* planting them with deadly but unconscious naïveté, a child lisping in banderillos for the banderillos came.

During the last few years, especially, there has been an entire chorus depreciating Hemingway's understanding. Raised first among the more serious reviews, the cry was swelled by emulative pipings from even the daily book-gossipers; it reached a climax of comic fatuity in the solemn judgment of one of these that "as a thinking being he has a very great deal to learn." Sometimes by dogma, sometimes by derision, Hemingway's claims to everything except a kind of instinctive flair for writing have been denied and the log-

From Edgar Johnson, "Farewell the Separate Peace: The Rejections of Ernest Hemingway." First published in the *Sewanee Review*, vol. 48, no. 3, Summer 1940. Reprinted with permission of the *Sewanee Review*.

ical integrity of his work misunderstood. It would be persuasive but it would be an error to seek the roots of these misjudgments in political feeling. They already existed in germ long before Hemingway ever fought for loyalist Spain, long before he had any politics except the rejection of politics; and even now they may be uncovered in journals of every shade of opinion. The reasons lie rather, I believe, in the fact that Hemingway is an intellectual who has renounced intellectualism.

Writers in our time may safely attack almost all things, save only the intellectual and his values. They may sneer at Main Street and howl against Wall Street, they may mutter darkly against the perfection of the Constitution, they may even snipe at the outworks of learning and science. But let a writer defame the holy of holies, intellectualism itself, and he is torn to shreds by all the feline tongues of the intelligentsia, male and female together. Aldous Huxley, to be sure, impaled them upon the sharpened stakes of satire and escaped untorn—at least, until his current phase pacifist mysticism—but largely because his very attack implied an altitude of brow so much loftier than even high-browism as to reaffirm its essential values. Hemingway, however, like D.H. Lawrence, has quarreled, although not so fundamentally and all-inclusively, with the root-assumptions of bohemian-aesthetic intellectualism. And like Lawrence he has been derided as a sort of modern Heidelberg Man, incapable of understanding the things he despised.

Hemingway is himself partly responsible for these misapprehensions. He has sympathetically portrayed simple and ignorant people: prizefighters, matadors, boys, jockeys, whores, bartenders, waiters. He has savagely mauled the futile crew of post-War expatriates and perverts and pseudo-literary sophisticates, the wealthy and the idle and the vicious, drifting from bar to brothel in Paris, Madrid, New York, and Florida. A skilled amateur boxer, he has almost paraded a rather fractious muscular virility and laid himself open to a good deal of kidding about hair on the chest, to which he has responded with an angry and humorless bellicosity. He has breathed a lot of fiery sentiments about bulls, blood, and death, and a good deal of truculence about his fellow-craftsmen.

None of these facts, however, really makes Hemingway the chest-pounding atavism of the caricatures. Neither brawn nor the scorn of bad writers implies absence of brain. It is rather simple-minded to assume that only the simple-minded can sympathize with or understand the simple. It is rather worse than that to read Hemingway's satire on sophistication as the howl of a savage against what he cannot comprehend.

If Hemingway rejected obvious subtlety and repudiated high-browism he rejected them not through incapacity but comprehension, rejected them in a way because rejection has been the principle of his intellectual growth. Indeed, Hemingway's development as a writer has been almost dialectical: thesis followed by rejecting antithesis, the resolving synthesis fusing the values of its predecessors, and then being rejected in turn as Hemingway worked through its flaws. Its stages should be sufficient to refute those critics who find in his career "evidence of no mental growth whatever.". . .

## ANTITHESES REJECTED

Three kinds of rejection that Hemingway has previously dealt with are posed in *To Have and Have Not*: the intelligent rejection of the merely biological plane of living, the sophisticated rejection of all responsibility except that of self-indulgence and having a good time, and the philosophic or heroic rejection of letting the world go its ways and standing for personal ties alone. The simple and the ignorant, the instinctive and unreflective, are always defeated in the end because they do not understand. Hemingway can respect and like them, as he always has; he sees that their strength is not enough. And yet their virtues are precisely what the sophisticated have lost: "The simplicity which is so large an element in a noble nature," as Thucydides observed, "was laughed to death and vanished out of the world." To the third way of rejection we shall presently return.

Hemingway's satire on the sophisticates and writers is bitterer than ever before. The fat bohemian tourists at Freddie's bar, Richard Gordon shoddily following the latest literary fashions by writing a novel about a strike in a garment factory, and leaving his Helen while he goes off to tea and fornication with a wealthy nymphomaniac whose husband looks on shadowily from the doorway, the homosexual musicians and yachtsmen, the wife of a drug-consuming movie director taking refuge in self-abuse while her lover is lost in drunken slumber: the illustrations mount to pure horror.

The revulsion reaches its peak in Helen's denunciation of Richard and of love: "Love is all the dirty little tricks you taught me that you probably got out of some book. I'm through with you and I'm through with love. Your kind of picknose love. You writer." And all the end of the book is full of desperation and doom, of suicide in the background, people taking "the long drop", shooting themselves with automatics, "those admirable instruments ... so well-designed to end the American dream when it becomes a nightmare." But if there is horror, there is pity too: Professor McWalsey pitying Richard Gordon, Hemingway pitying his own characters, as McWalsey goes back to his bar saying, "I will now return to the anaesthetic I have used for seventeen years and will not need much longer."

Against these spiritual failures we have the strength, tenderness, courage, ingenuity, and manhood of Harry Morgan. In him are fused the qualities of all those figures with whom Hemingway has formerly stood, and added to them, a heroic stature. But even heroic stature Hemingway finds insufficient; and in this last rejection—and it *is* rejection, for all his admiration for Harry Morgan—Hemingway reaches a logical affirmation transcending negation.

The simple brave had fought, but they had never understood. Jake [*The Sun Also Rises*] had been made a passive onlooker by a physical mutilation. Henry [*A Farewell to Arms*] had seen and reflected and tried to stand aside, but had been caught, by his very humanity, within the trap. Morgan is almost as simple and nonreflective as Manuel Garcia ["The Undefeated"], and, like him, he is undefeated because he is not broken. Like Jake and Henry, however, he has taken the measure of the world—not pessimistically or philosophically, but almost without thinking about it, and gone through life standing alone, for himself, his wife, and their girls. But unlike Henry, he fights the world; it is by trying to win a separate victory that he seeks a separate peace.

And it is this very isolation, as Hemingway now perceives, that has ensured disaster. Harry Morgan does not know it, but the materially well-fed and voracious, riding prosperous, very victorious, and fighting for themselves alone as much as he, are in reality even more defeated. Hemingway has drawn together all his threads, and realized that it was the very core of his earlier positions, the separate peace, that needed to be rejected. Morgan sees the light before the end, while the light is fading from his eyes, and he does not blame the universe. He sees now that he has been beaten because he has tried to stand alone and fight alone: "'One man alone ain't got. No man alone now.' He stopped. 'No matter how a man alone ain't got no bloody . . . chance.'" "It had taken him a long while to get it out," Hemingway concludes, "and it had taken him all his life to learn it." But it is the logical climax of Hemingway's development. It is true, as various critics have pointed out, that his counterpoint in *To Have and Have Not* is not entirely successful. He fails to bring his two worlds together. Harry Morgan and the sophisticates touch, but they do not intermingle. And Harry's realization of the reason for his having had a hopeless struggle all his life is too sudden and too unprepared for. Nevertheless *To Have and Have Not* is a better book than almost any of the critics have allowed. The earlier chapters, both those where Morgan speaks for himself and those where Hemingway reveals him in action and dialogue, the fishing scenes, the chink smuggling, the warm, strong, and tender relation with Marie, are among the best writing Hemingway has ever done; they build up the picture of the man with an assurance and solidity that Hemingway has never excelled. And his bohemian wastrels and weaklings, mere sketches as all of them are save Richard and Helen Gordon, are more truly lost than any he has portrayed before. Seen with a bitter and mournful pity, they are indeed the hollow men, wandering in despair or jerking galvanically through the mists of Hades, a gray world of doom.

It is not they, however, who convey the tone of the book, but Harry Morgan, given the clue to victory even in the hour of defeat.

# Hemingway's Men and (the Absence of) Women

Leslie Fiedler

Hemingway is only comfortable when writing about "men without women," observes Leslie Fiedler, author of *Love and Death in the American Novel.* In his more ambitious fiction he does try to create female characters, but his women are generally of two types: dark and subservient or Anglo-Saxon and threatening. These characters are never quite human. Brett Ashley in *The Sun Also Rises* comes closer than most, but Brett's individuality comes from her refusal to become "feminine," and none of her relationships with men are satisfactory.

Hemingway is much addicted to describing the sex act. It is the symbolic center of his work: a scene to which he recurs when nostalgically evoking his boyhood as "Up in Michigan"; illustrating the virtues of the sturdy poor as in *To Have and Have Not*; reflecting on civil strife and heroism as in *For Whom the Bell Tolls*; or projecting the fantasies of a man facing old age as in *Across the River and Into the Trees.* There are, however, no *women* in his books! In his earlier fictions, Hemingway's descriptions of the sexual encounter are intentionally brutal, in his later ones unintentionally comic; for in no case can he quite succeed in making his females human, and coitus performed with an animal, a thing, or a wet dream is either horrible or ridiculous. If in *For Whom the Bell Tolls* Hemingway has written the most absurd love scene in the history of the American novel, this is not because he lost momentarily his skill and authority; it is a give-away—a moment which illuminates the whole erotic content of his fiction.

Hemingway is only really comfortable in dealing with

"men without women." The relations of father to son, of bat-
tle-companions, friends on a fishing trip, fellow inmates in a
hospital, a couple of waiters preparing to close up shop, a
bullfighter and his manager, a boy and a gangster: these
move him to simplicity and truth. Perhaps he is best of all
with men who stand alone—in night-time scenes when the
solitary individual sweats in his bed on the verge of nightmare, or arises to confront himself in the glass; though he is
at home, too, with the Rip Van Winkle archetype, with men
in flight from women. Certainly, he returns again and again
to the fishing trip and the journey to the war—those two traditional evasions of domesticity and civil life. Yet he feels an
obligation to introduce women into his more ambitious fictions, though he does not know what to do with them beyond taking them to bed. All his life, he has been haunted by
a sense of how simple it all was once, when he could take
his Indian girl into the clean-smelling woods, stretch out be-
side her on the pine-needles (her brother standing guard),
and rise to no obligations at all. In a story called "Fathers
and Sons," he writes a tribute to that prototypical, mindless,
undemanding, scarcely human girl: "Could you say she did
first what no one has ever done better and mention plump
brown legs, flat belly, hard little breasts, well holding arms,
quick searching tongue, the flat eyes, the good taste of mouth
. . . and hemlock needles stuck against your belly. . . . Long
time ago good. Now no good."

## A REJECTION OF MATURITY

In Hemingway the rejection of the sentimental happy ending
of marriage involves the acceptance of the sentimental
happy beginning of innocent and inconsequential sex, and
camouflages the rejection of maturity and of fatherhood itself. The only story in which he portrays a major protagonist
as having a child is the one in which he remembers with
nostalgia his little Trudy of the "well holding arms, quick
searching tongue," and looks forward to the time when his
son will have a gun and they can pop off to the forest like two
boys together. More typically he aspires to be not Father but
"Papa," the Old Man of the girl-child with whom he is tem-
porarily sleeping; and surely there is no writer to whom
childbirth more customarily presents itself as the essential
catastrophe. At best he portrays it as a plaguey sort of accident which forces a man to leave his buddies behind at the

moment of greatest pleasure as in "Cross Country Snow"; at worst, it becomes in his fiction that horror which drives the tender-hearted husband of "Indian Camp" to suicide, or which takes Catherine away from Lieutenant Henry in *A Farewell to Arms.*

Poor things, all they wanted was innocent orgasm after orgasm on an island of peace in a world at war, love-making without end in a scarcely real country to which neither owed life or allegiance. But such a relationship can, of course, never last, as Hemingway–Nick Adams–Lieutenant Henry has always known: "They all ended the same. Long time ago good. Now no good." Only the dead woman becomes neither a bore nor a mother; and before Catherine can quite become either she must die, killed not by Hemingway, of course, but by childbirth! It is all quite sad and lovely at the end: the last kiss bestowed on what was a woman and is now a statue, the walk home through the rain. Poe himself could not have done better, though he was haunted not by the memory of a plump little Indian on the hemlock needles but a fantasy of a high-born maiden "loved with a love that was more than love" and carried away by death.

## DARK LADY VS. FAIR LADY

Had Catherine lived, she could only have turned into a bitch; for this is the fate in Hemingway's imagination of all Anglo-Saxon women. In him, the cliché of Dark Lady and Fair survives, but stood on its head, exactly reversed. The Dark Lady, who is neither wife nor mother, blends with the image of Fayaway, the exotic servant-consort reconstructed by Melville in *Typee* out of memories of an eight-year-old Polynesian girl-child. In Hemingway, such women are mindless, soft, subservient; painless devices for extracting seed without human engagement. The Fair Lady, on the other hand, who gets pregnant and wants a wedding, or uses her sexual allure to assert her power, is seen as a threat and a destroyer of men. But the seed-extractors are Indians or Latins, black-eyed and dusky in hue, while the castrators are at least Anglo-Saxon if not symbolically blond. Neither are permitted to be virgins; indeed, both are imagined as having been often possessed, though in the case of the Fair Woman promiscuity is used as a device for humiliating and unmanning the male foolish enough to have entered into a marriage with her. Through the Dark anti-virgin, on the other hand, a new lover enters into a blameless communion with the other uncommitted males who have possessed her and departed, as well as with those yet to come. It is a kind of homosexuality once-removed, the appeal of the whorehouse (Eden of the world of men without women) embodied in a single figure.

## A CURIOUS ATTITUDE TOWARD WOMEN

The hero's whole attitude toward women is curious. It is either warlike or sentimental. He started out rejecting his mother in defense of his father, and since then the partners Hemingway has drawn for him are either vicious, destructive wives like Macomber's ["The Short Happy Life of Francis Macomber"], or daydreams like Catherine [*A Farewell to Arms*], Maria [*For Whom the Bell Tolls*], and Renata [*Across the River and into the Trees*], the most recent version of the ideal. More than Catherine, though rather less than Renata, Maria is just too ethereal for the world she is in—is submissive and devoted beyond credibility and to the extinction of her own character. She does not like to drink (that's for Men); she exists for her lover alone, and has no other interest or function in all life or the world but to serve him. And although she is for a while a very lovely vision, as we get to know her she becomes more and more a vision until ultimately she ceases to be a person at all.

Philip Young, *Ernest Hemingway*, 1952.

When Hemingway's bitches are Americans, they are hopeless and unmitigated bitches; symbols of Home and Mother as remembered by the boy who could never forgive Mama for having wantonly destroyed Papa's Indian collection! Mrs. Macomber, who, in "The Short Happy Life of Francis Macomber," kills her husband for having alienated the affections of the guide with whom she is having one of her spiteful little affairs, is a prime example of the type. And "the woman," in "The Snows of Kilimanjaro" another, who with her wealth has weaned her husband from all that sustained his virility, betrayed him to aimlessness and humiliation. Like Fitzgerald's betrayed men, he can choose only to die, swoon to the death he desires at the climax of a dream of escape.

The British bitch is for Hemingway only a demi-bitch, however, as the English are only, as it were, demi-Americans.

Catherine is delivered from her doom by death; Brett Ashley in *The Sun Also Rises* (1926) is permitted, once at least, the gesture of herself rejecting her mythical role. But it is quite a feat at that, and Brett cannot leave off congratulating herself: "You know it makes one feel rather good deciding not to be a bitch." Yet Brett never becomes a woman really; she is mythicized rather than redeemed. And if she is the most satisfactory female character in all of Hemingway, this is because for once she is presented not as an animal or as a nightmare but quite audaciously as a goddess, the bitch-goddess with a boyish bob (Hemingway is rather fond of women who seem as much boy as girl), the Lilith of the '20's. No man embraces her without being in some sense castrated, except for Jake Barnes who is unmanned to begin with; no man approaches her without *wanting* to be castrated, except for Romero, who thinks naïvely that she is—or can easily become—a woman. Indeed, when Brett leaves that nineteen-year-old bullfighter, one suspects that, though she avows it is because she will not be "one of those bitches who ruins children," she is really running away because she thinks he might *make* her a woman. Certainly, Romero's insistence that she let her hair grow out has something to do with it: "He wanted me to grow my hair out. Me, with long hair. I'd look so like hell. . . . He said it would make me more womanly. I'd look a fright."

To yield up her cropped head would be to yield up her emancipation from female servitude, to become feminine rather than phallic; and this Brett cannot do. She thinks of herself as a flapper, though the word perhaps would not have occurred to her, as a member of the "Lost Generation"; but the Spaniards know her immediately as a terrible goddess, the avatar of an ancient archetype. She tries in vain to enter into the circle of Christian communion, but is always turned aside at the door; she changes her mind, she has forgotten her hat—the apparent reason never matters; she belongs to a world alien and prior to that of the Christian churches in which Jake finds a kind of peace. In Pamplona, Brett is surrounded by a group of *riau-riau* dancers, who desert a religious procession to follow her, set her up as a rival to Saint Fermin: "Some dancers formed a circle around Brett and started to dance. They wore big wreaths of white garlic around their necks. . . . They were all chanting. Brett wanted to dance but they did not want her to. They wanted her as an image to dance around." Incapable of love except as a moment in bed, Brett can bestow on her worshipers nothing more than the brief joy of a drunken ecstasy—followed by suffering and deprivation and regret. In the end, not only are her physical lovers unmanned and degraded, but even Jake, who is her priest and is protected by his terrible wound, is humiliated. For her service is a betrayal not only of his Catholic faith but of his pure passion for bullfighting and trout-fishing; and the priest of the bitch-goddess is, on the purely human level, a pimp.

# A Strange Kind of Romance

## Stanley Cooperman

Most of Hemingway's commentators agree that his protagonists—especially Frederick Henry in *A Farewell to Arms*—are "romantic." But Stanley Cooperman, author of *World War I and the American Novel*, points out that when the emasculated Frederick Henry turns to his newfound love-object, Catherine, "romance" becomes an elusive concept. Catherine serves a role that is more a healer than a lover. By being completely passive, she tries to restore to him the initiative that Hemingway feels is essential to masculinity. But her passivity reduces Frederick Henry's love to a kind of narcissism. The author's treatment of love—like his treatment of death—betrays his own fear of the full spectrum of experience.

"Byronic," says Alfred Kazin of Frederic Henry and *A Farewell to Arms*, and the view of Hemingway's protagonist as a neo-Romantic lover has long been with us. George Snell dismisses the love story of *A Farewell to Arms* as "not only trite but so sentimentalized as to be almost preposterous"; Edmund Wilson speaks of Hemingway's "amoeba like" women; E.B. Burgum refers to "colorless banality"; Francis Hackett sneers at Catherine as a "divine lollipop"; Isaac Rosenfeld notes "the perpetual adolescence of the emotions to cover a fear, and subsequent hatred, of adolescent love"; while Carl Van Doren more optimistically sees a romantic emancipation from the old duality of flesh vs. spirit ("if both were fused the mind might draw strength from the body and hold its head up in self-respect and joy"). Whether for praise or blame, most of Hemingway's commentators have agreed that "romance" of one sort or another defines his protagonists in general and Frederic Henry in particular.

From Stanley Cooperman, "Death and *Cojones*: Hemingway's *A Farewell to Arms*," *South Atlantic Quarterly*, vol. 63, no. 1, Winter 1964, pp. 85-92. Copyright Duke University Press, 1964. Reprinted with permission.

What this "romance" represents, however, remains obscure; the word itself is one of those quicksilver epithets often handled and seldom fixed. Perhaps the best clue to the basic "romance" of Frederic Henry is to be found not in criticism, but in the remarks of Rinaldi in *A Farewell to Arms*—Rinaldi, who refuses to take Frederic Henry's value-through-love seriously, who deflates his sudden solemnity, and who dances a jig of verbal mockery around the very bedside of the New Redemption: "'I know, you are the fine Anglo-Saxon boy,' Rinaldi says. 'I know, I will wait till I see the Anglo-Saxon brushing away harlotry with a toothbrush. . . . All my life I encounter sacred objects, but very few with you. I suppose you must have them too.'" For Rinaldi is not impressed with the new-found passion of his friend. He is disappointed. And the reason for his disappointment is the fact that he sees Frederic Henry as dependent upon that very crutch of Protestant sexuality from which he had assumed this American to be exempt.

Hemingway's protagonist, indeed, with his sense of manhood shattered by technological rape ("'I was blown up while we were eating cheese'"), turns toward his "lovely cool goddess" because there is nothing else. Deprived of that initiative so essential to Hemingway's concept of virility, unable to ritualize his role in the war so as to act rather than be acted upon, threatened with the horror of male passivity, Frederic Henry is reduced to the "worship" Rinaldi so ironically defines. Action and violence, once simple, have become complex, and would master Frederic Henry rather than be mastered by him. For this reason Catherine does indeed become "sacred"; only through her mirror-surface, her renunciation of self, can Henry once again take comfort from the reflection of his own face.

## MEDICATION, NOT ROMANCE

Only a love-object, in other words, an erotic shadow shaped by passivity, can return to Frederic Henry the initiative essential to his manhood. Catherine offers to become "'whatever you want'"—and this is what the war, what voluntary violence itself, should have been and was not. From the moment that violence and action intrude upon Frederic Henry's will, from the moment that they cease to exist merely by virtue of his consent (as they do exist in Hemingway's later work by virtue of the bullfighter's consent, or the hunter's, or the fisherman's), his relationship with Catherine becomes far more vital than a "chess-game" of idle fornication; its urgency and inviolability are shaped by a pursuit of an absolute psychic need. For Frederic Henry does not require romance from Catherine, but medication, and in this respect he is less the Byronic lover than patient. Catherine, who is simply there at his disposal, permits him his masculine role: action determined and made necessary by nothing beyond its own will. And when this last cure also proves illusory, when Catherine asserts her own individuality by the very act of dying, there is nothing left of manhood at all. Frederic Henry takes his final walk into the rain as a sort of Jake Barnes, who in *The Sun Also Rises* stares blankly at the mirror of his own impotence. The hyena of passivity—always a nightmare for Hemingway—reduces Frederic Henry to a spiritual *castrado.*

Essential to this emasculation is the inability to handle any quality of *otherness* except in terms of ritualization. The other—whether animate or inanimate—is tolerable only insofar as it can be manipulated, controlled as one controls the trout line, the bullfight, the hunt, or the female—who achieves her own "truth" and "purity" by becoming an object. Since any experience that is an extension of self holds no terror, only those experiences that are extensions of self may be absorbed (or mastered). Even death, providing it can be arranged and patterned, may serve as an exercise in virility; only when death refuses to be patterned, when action—impersonal if not antipersonal—becomes its own perpetuator, does flight into other areas of experience become an undignified and involuntary imperative. There is no question of *cojones*, of will, among those soldiers groveling and "choking through the whole attack" in "Champs d'Honneur" (written while the war experience was still all too fresh in Hemingway's mind). What Frederick J. Hoffman sees as the "violation" or "traumatic shock" of technological war is a vital aspect not only in the relationship between Frederic Henry and Catherine, but in the literary career of Hemingway himself.

Unpatterned, unritualized, and other, the war intrudes upon Frederic Henry and therefore is bad; Catherine never intrudes, never seizes the initiative, and so is "good." It is such "purity" that Rinaldi, the ubiquitous and clever diagnostician, so thoroughly distrusts; "'You never know if the girl will really like it,'" he churlishly remarks. Catherine has become too completely an object; her very desire is "pure" for Frederic Henry because it creates narcissism ('"I want what you want ... there isn't any me any more, just what you want'"). The total effect, indeed, is something more; it is autoerotic. For only the autoerotic image, love without the other, can be counted upon not to change, not to escape into complexity, not to threaten, and not to break into the controlled act by thrusting forward a pattern of its own.

## RITUAL AGAINST FEAR

All depends upon the mystique of ritual, even art itself; for this reason Hemingway's language conveys that peculiar sense of caution, wariness, and deliberation which so belies its own realistic surface. Although there is no doubt that a reaction against the rhetoric of the Great Crusade [World War I as a "call to glory"] powerfully affected Hemingway's style, Harry Levin's reference to his "verbal skepticism" explains the particular quality of that style only partially. It is not skepticism that underlies ritual, but fear—fear of the unknown or unmanageable. In the bull ring men can defeat death even while dying because they surround it with form: the initiative, in a very real sense, remains theirs. As a bulwark against passivity, ritual—whether in the temple, the bedroom, the arena, or the battlefield—has been one of humanity's basic psychological needs, and it is in this sense that Hemingway so carefully, indeed so compulsively arranges and limits experience. Technological warfare eliminated the battlefield as a resource for ritual, while flabby rhetoric and political opportunism eliminated the temple. Only love remained, but very briefly and very deceptively: Catherine, after all, shattered Frederic Henry's ritual by dying quite without his consent. And after love too has been "spoiled" there is only the arena, a resource for Hemingway throughout his subsequent career.

Ritualized language and prescribed limitation of experience to be rendered or even talked about may produce honest and precise writing. Despite all the insistence on precision and virility, however, there is in Hemingway's work an almost maidenish fear of the full spectrum of potentialities within experience. This is particularly true of love, and it is with reference to love as an alternative to meaningful action, unmistakable choice, or virile death that Hemingway's dietetic art can become so inadequate that it may seem a parody of its own virtues. While action and ritual can be rendered by his type of art, person or process cannot; for this reason Catherine (as Rinaldi understands) becomes a leaf of lettuce nibbled by a man on a mountain top where the only sound he hears is the sound of his own teeth. There is no flavor here, and little flesh either. Frederic Henry's lettuce-woman may leave him always hungry, no matter how much he takes of her, but this insatiability is due less to a virile appetite than to a lack of substance-to-be-consumed. It is a measure of the book's essential Puritanism (rather than romance) that autoeroticism becomes the "clean," the "pure," the "true," and the desperate analgesic for reduced manhood. A world of violence has rejected all the rituals of love and violence alike, and the result is total defeat. . . .

The loss of initiative represented by technological violence and the attempt to regain this initiative through the bedroom or the arena are basic elements in *A Farewell to Arms* and Hemingway's later work. The war itself, certainly, represents a break in the continuum from natural violence in the northwoods to ritualized violence in the bull ring; it is the one area where death cannot be mastered through the assertion of will, the ritual of *cojones,* and for this reason it threatens rather than fulfills what Alfred Kazin calls "the individual's fierce unassailable pride in his pride"—virility itself. For pride is impossible when no choice is offered, when the initiative is stolen, and Hemingway tends to avoid rather than confront any experience where initiative becomes external. Confrontation, indeed, is a theme of Hemingway's work only in a special and very limited sense: his protagonists attempt to confront death in terms of ritual or they refuse to confront it at all.

This dependence upon ritual, and consequent horror when the impossibility of ritualizing reduces the individual to passivity, indicates that Hemingway's preoccupation with death is something far removed from existential confrontation. That so many critics have indeed read Hemingway in existential terms is due to a double failure of perception: first, the failure to perceive that technological violence in World War I deprived death of any "moment of truth" whatsoever; and, second, that a World War I protagonist like Frederic Henry, "'blown up while we were eating cheese,'" becomes a refugee from precisely that form of obliteration, of *nada*, he no longer can master. . . .

Hemingway's ritual of death, possible only outside rather than within modern war, is escape rather than confrontation; when the ritual is not possible, there is no confrontation at all. Like the Hemingway love relationship (which, when it is "good," is always between a man and his shadow and so avoids the threat—and the reality—of the other), Hemingway's ritual is both formal and abstract, and so represents a retreat from rather than acceptance of existential absurdity. This is the real meaning of the World War I experience (death without ritual), and it explains why Hemingway afterward was successful only in those areas where ritual became possible: the bullfight, the safari, the fishing trip. For post–World War II existentialism, however, ritual for its own sake is no more acceptable a formula—precisely because it is a formula—than art for the sake of art; the illusions of ritual do not truly confront and defeat death any more than a cocktail party confronts and defeats human isolation.

Too many critics have failed to realize, or remember, the enormous difference for Hemingway between World War I death and the death which either preceded it (death in the woods) or followed it (ritual death in the bull ring). John Killinger, indeed, in *Hemingway and the Dead Gods*, sees no difference at all: "In the blinding flash of a shell, in the icy-burning impact of a bullet, in the dangerous vicinity of a wounded lion, in the contact of a bull's horn, in that ill-defined twilight between life and imminent death where time and place are irrelevant questions, man faces his freedom." But Frederic Henry knows better. There was neither "choice" nor "freedom" for him, no reason for medals or even talk; he was "eating cheese"; he was totally—almost obscenely—*done to*; he was, as Frederick Hoffman remarks, "violated"; his experience was emasculatory because passive and therefore feminine. "Soldiers never do die well," Hemingway tells us in "Champs d'Honneur," and his entire career as a writer was in a vital sense a search for those areas where a man can at least maintain the illusion of making love to death rather than being violated by it.

# CHAPTER 3

# The Hemingway Style

READINGS ON
ERNEST HEMINGWAY

# Art as Survival

Alfred Kazin

In Hemingway's fatalistic view, writing—his art—
was his major defense against the meaninglessness
of life, writes literary critic Alfred Kazin. He explains
that Hemingway sought a new kind of prose that
would be capable of expressing "the real thing" even
beyond the third dimension. If, as an artist, he could
perfectly convey the description of natural fact in
such a new dimension, he could rise above "that
confusion which was half the terror of living."

"What do you think happens to people who aren't artists?
What do you think people who aren't artists become?"

"I feel they don't become: I feel nothing happens to them; I
feel negation becomes of them."

—E.E. Cummings, Introduction to *The Enormous Room*

As E.E. Cummings saw it, the world was composed of brutal
sensations and endured only by a fiercely desperate courage
and love; it was so anarchical that all attempts to impose
order were motivated by either ignorance or chicanery.
What remained to the artist, who was always the special victim of this world, was the pride of individual self-knowledge
and the skill that went beyond all the revolutionary and sentimental illusions of a possible fraternity among men and
gave all its devotion to the integrity of art.

A parallel code of fatalism developed in Ernest Hemingway's hands into the freshest and most deliberate art of the
day. What Cummings had suggested in his embittered war
autobiography was that the postwar individual, first as soldier and citizen, now as artist, was the special butt of the
universe. As Wyndham Lewis wrote later of the typical Hemingway hero, he was the man "things are done to." To Hemingway life became supremely the task of preserving oneself
by preserving and refining one's art. Art was the ultimate, as
it was perhaps the only, defense. In a society that served only

to prey upon the individual, endurance was possible only by retaining one's identity and thus proclaiming one's valor. Writing was not a recreation, it was a way of life; it was born of desperation and enmity and took its insights from a militant suffering. Yet it could exist only as it purified itself; it had meaning only as it served to tell the truth. A writer succeeded by proving himself superior to circumstance; his significance as an artist lay in his honesty, his courage, and the will to endure. Hemingway's vision of life, as John Peale Bishop put it, was thus one of perpetual annihilation. "Since the will can do nothing against circumstance, choice is precluded; those things are good which the senses report good; and beyond their brief record there is only the remorseless devaluation of nature."

---

## THE QUIVERING CORE OF HUMAN FEAR

For a moment of his career [in *The Sun Also Rises*], Hemingway saw the human condition in starkly honest postwar terms. He angrily brushed aside conventional palliatives, dismissed the shams of literary explanation, and obstinately risked what seemed absurdities and obscenities to reach the naked, raw, quivering core of human fear and hysteria. His overpowering honesty produced a work of art that is at the same time a literal ordering of a historical-emotional experience.

Frederick J. Hoffman, *The Twenties: American Writing in the Postwar Decade,* 1962.

---

The remarkable thing about Hemingway from the first was that he did not grow up to this rigid sense of tragedy, or would not admit that he had. The background of his first stories, *In Our Time*, was the last frontier of his Michigan boyhood, a mountainous region of forests and lakes against which he appeared as the inquisitive but tight-lipped youth—hard, curt, and already a little sad. With its carefully cultivated brutality and austerity, the sullen boy in *In Our Time* revealed a mind fixed in its groove. These stories of his youth, set against the superb evocation of war monotony and horror, elaborately contrived to give the violence of the Michigan woods and the violence of war an equal value in the reader's mind, summarized Hemingway's education. Their significance lay in the number of things the young Hemingway had already taken for granted; they were a youth's stricken responses to a brutal environment, and the responses seemed to become all. Just as the war in *A Farewell to Arms* was to seem less important than the sensations it provoked, so the landscape of *In Our Time* had meaning only as the youth had learned from it. For Hemingway in his early twenties, the criticism of society had gone so deep that life seemed an abstraction; it was something one discounted by instinct and distrusted by habit. It was a sequence of violent actions and mechanical impulses: the brutality of men in the Michigan woods, the Indian husband who cut his throat after watching his wife undergo a Caesarian with a jackknife, adolescent loneliness and exaltation, a punch-drunk boxer on the road. And always below that level of native memories, interspersed with passing sketches of gangsters and bullfights, lay the war.

> Nick sat against the wall of the church where they had dragged him to be clear of machine-gun fire in the street. Both legs stuck out awkwardly. He had been hit in the spine. His face was sweaty and dirty. The sun shone on his face. The day was very hot.... Two Austrian dead lay in the rubble in the shade of the house. Up the street were other dead.... Nick turned his head carefully and looked at Rinaldi. "Senta Rinaldi. Senta. You and me we've made a separate peace."

## THE PHASES OF THE HEMINGWAY HERO

The glazed face of the Hemingway hero, which in its various phases was to become, like Al Capone's, the face of a decade and to appear on a succession of soldiers, bullfighters, explorers, gangsters, and unhappy revolutionaries, emerged slowly but definitively in *In Our Time*. The hero's first reaction was surprise, to be followed immediately by stupor; life, like the war, is in its first phase heavy, graceless, sullen; the theme is sounded in the rape of Liz Coates by the hired man. Then the war became comic, a series of incongruities. "Everybody was drunk. The whole battery was drunk going along the road in the dark.... The lieutenant kept riding his horse out into the fields and saying to him: 'I'm drunk, I tell you, mon vieux. Oh, I am so soused.'... It was funny going along that road." Then the whole affair became merely sordid, a huddle of refugees in the mud, the empty and perpetual flow of rain, a woman bearing her child on the road. "It rained all through the evacuation." By the sheer accumulation of horrors, the final phase was reached, and the end was a deceptive callousness.

> We were in a garden at Mons. Young Buckley came in with
> his patrol from across the river. The first German I saw
> climbed up over the garden wall. We waited till he got one leg
> over and then potted him. He had so much equipment on and
> looked awfully surprised and fell down into the garden. Then
> three more came over further down the wall. We shot them.
> They all came just like that.

Hemingway's own values were stated explicitly in the
story called "Soldier's Home," where he wrote that "Krebs
acquired the nausea in regard to experience that is the result
of untruth or exaggeration." The Hemingway archetype had
begun by contrasting life and war, devaluating one in terms
of the other. Now life became only another manifestation of
war; the Hemingway world is in a state of perpetual war. The
soldier gives way to the bullfighter, the slacker to the tired
revolutionary, the greed of war is identified with the corruption and violence of sport. Nothing remains but the individual's fierce unassailable pride in his pride, the will to go on,
the need to write without "untruth or exaggeration." As a soldier, he had preserved his sanity by rebelling quietly and
alone; he had made the separate peace. Mutiny was the last
refuge of the individual caught in the trap of war; chronic
mutiny now remains the safeguard of the individual in that
state of implicit belligerence between wars that the world
calls peace. The epos of death has become life's fundamental
narrative; the new hero is the matador in Chapter XII of *In
Our Time*. "When he started to kill it was all in the same
rush. The bull looking at him straight in front, hating. He
drew out the sword from the folds of the muleta and sighted
with the same movement and called to the bull, Toro! Toro!
and the bull charged and Villalta charged and just for a moment they became one." The casual grace of the bullfighter,
which at its best is an esthetic passion, is all. And even that
grace may become pitiful, as in the saga of the aging matador in "The Undefeated." For the rest, defeat and corruption
and exhaustion lie everywhere: marriage in "Cross-Country
Snow," sport in "My Old Man" ("Seems like when they get
started they don't leave a guy nothing"), the gangrene of Fascism in "Che Ti Dice la Patria?" The climax of that first exercise in disillusion is reached in the terse and bitter narrative
called "The Revolutionist," the story of the young boy who
had been tortured by the Whites in Budapest when the Soviet
collapsed, and who found Italy in 1919 beautiful. "In spite of
Hungary, he believed altogether in the world revolution."

"But how is the movement going in Italy?" he asked.
"Very badly," I said.
"But it will go better," he said. "You have everything here.
It is the one country that every one is sure of. It will be the
starting point of everything."

## THE SEARCH FOR AN INTENSELY PRECISE PROSE

. . . Hemingway's intense search for "the real thing" ["the sequence of motion and fact which made the emotion and
which would be as valid in a year or ten years or, with luck
and if you stated it purely enough, always"] had already sin-
gled him out in Paris before he published *In Our Time*. In
those early years, guided by his interest in poetry and his
experiences as a reporter of the European debacle, he
seemed to be feeling his way toward a new prose, a prose
that would be not only absolutely true to the events reported
and to the accent of common speech, but would demand of
itself an original evocativeness and plasticity. What he
wanted, as he said later in *Death in the Afternoon*, was a
prose more intensely precise than conventional prose, and
hence capable of effects not yet achieved. He wanted to see
"how far prose can be carried if anyone is serious enough
and has luck. There is a fourth and fifth dimension that can
be gotten. . . . It is much more difficult than poetry. It is prose
that has never been written. But it can be written without
tricks and without cheating. With nothing that will go bad
afterwards." Yet what he was aiming at in one sense, F.O.
Matthiessen has pointed out, was the perfect yet poetic nat-
uralness of a Thoreau. Hemingway's surface affiliations as a
prose craftsman were with his first teachers, Gertrude Stein
and Sherwood Anderson, who taught him the requisite simplicity and fidelity and—Gertrude Stein more than Anderson—an ear for the natural rhythms of speech. But his
deeper associations went beyond them, beyond even the
Flaubertian tradition of discipline and *le mot juste* [the exact,
appropriate word]. He did not want to write "artistic prose,"
and Gertrude Stein and Anderson, equally joined in their hatred of display and their search for an inner truth in prose,
had certainly taught him not to. But he wanted not merely to
tell "the truth about his own feelings at the moment when
they exist"; he wanted to aim at that luminous and imaginative truth which a writer like Thoreau, on the strength of a
muscular integrity and passion for nature very like his own,

had created out of a monumental fidelity to the details of life as he saw them. What he wanted was that sense of grace, that "sequence of motion and fact" held at unwavering pitch, that could convey, as nothing else could, the secret fluid symbolism in the facts touched and recorded. . . .

It was in his unceasing quest of a conscious perfection through style that Hemingway proclaimed his distinction. To tell what had happened, as he wrote later, one used "one trick or another," dialogue being the supreme trick. But "the real thing," the pulse of his art, was to Hemingway from the first that perfect blending of fact into symbol, that perfect conversion of natural rhythm into an evocation of the necessary emotion, that would fuse the various phases of contemporary existence—love, war, sport—and give them a collective grace. And it was here that style and experience came together for him. Man endured the cruelty and terror of life only by the sufferance of his senses and his occasional enjoyment of them; but in that sufferance and enjoyment, if only he could convey them perfectly, lay the artist's special triumph. He could rise above the dull submissive sense of outrage which most men felt in the face of events. By giving a new dimension to the description of natural fact, he could gain a refuge from that confusion which was half the terror of living. What this meant was brilliantly illustrated in the association of the worlds of peace and war in *In Our Time*; the theme of universal loneliness in the midst of war that was sounded in the very first paragraph of *A Farewell to Arms* and attained its classic expression in the retreat at Caporetto, where the flowing river, the long grumbling line of soldiers, the officers who are being shot together by the carabinieri, seem to melt together in the darkness; the extraordinary scene in *The Sun Also Rises* where Robert Cohn, sitting with Jake and his friends at the bullfight, is humiliated a moment before the steer is gored in the ring. In each case the animal in man has found its parallel and key in some event around it; the emotion has become the fact.

If "the real thing" could not always be won, or retained after it had been won, there were other forms of grace—the pleasures of drinking and making love, the stabbing matador dancing nervously before his bull, the piercing cry of the hunt, the passionate awareness of nature that would allow a man to write a sentence like "In shooting quail you must not get between them, or when they flush they will come pouring at you, some rising steep, some skimming by your ears, whirring into a size you have never seen them in the air as they pass." If art was an expression of fortitude, fortitude at its best had the quality of art. Beyond fortitude, which even in *For Whom the Bell Tolls* is the pride of a professional integrity and skill, there was the sense of nature paralyzed, nature frozen into loneliness or terror. No nature writer in all American literature save Thoreau has had Hemingway's sensitiveness to color, to climate, to the knowledge of physical energy under heat or cold, that knowledge of the body thinking and moving through a landscape that Edmund Wilson, in another connection, has called Hemingway's "barometric accuracy." That accuracy was the joy of the huntsman and the artist; beyond that and its corresponding gratifications, Hemingway seemed to attach no value to anything else. There were only absolute values or absolute degradations.

# A Focus on the Immediate and the Human in *A Farewell to Arms*

Jay Gellens

Playwright and editor Jay Gellens observes that *A Farewell to Arms* examines the drama of reasonable people caught up in the absurdity of war. Hemingway focuses throughout on the concrete details of his characters' lives in the midst of chaos. The hero's concentration on the rich sensory details of his life and his love story (which would be just a normal, everyday series of events in peacetime) for a time brings a sense of freshness to a world at war—or at least "stops the room from whirling" for a while.

Critics of *A Farewell to Arms* acknowledge unanimously the fine density of its texture, the power of its understatement, the toughness of its irony. Searching for its further significance, they have either extrapolated a variety of symbolic machineries, or denied that any exist. From the latter point of view, the novel is no more than a story of two lovers flattened by the obscenity of the war, their doom periodically interrupted by a series of exercises in the acute rendering of the physical world, their philosophical peaks shining through a few clichés about burning ants, baseball, and getting "strong at the broken places."

We can, however, observe certain obsessive patterns in the novel's treatment of the love affair, the war, the natural world, and the fate that inscrutably directs, or fails to direct, it all. Hemingway's initial portraits of the surgeon and the priest suggest the book's preoccupation with the drama of reasonable men caught up in the absurdity of a world at war. The surgeon practices his obsolete Sisyphian skill with stoic resignation—he is calm, still enjoys the pleasures of wine and prostitution, and even aspires toward a lost innocence in his comradeship with Henry and his solicitude for the first fumbling rituals of the love affair.

The priest's commitment is, in another way, more viciously refuted by the environment of war. If the surgeon's skill is disqualified by an operation that will never have time enough to heal, the priest's faith is undermined in the ruthless nihilism of the smoky cafes, where the only evidence of everlasting life is meaningless death. Yet he continues to defend his faith, exhorts Henry to go to the Abruzzi, "where the roads were frozen and hard as iron, where it was clear cold and dry and the snow was dry and powdery and hare-tracks in the snow . . . and there was good hunting," to undertake, perhaps, a mode of religious meditation which will clear his mind for the regeneration of his faith. . . .

## MORAL GROWTH TOWARD THE CODE

Robert Penn Warren has remarked the implicit ladder of moral growth toward the code in Hemingway's fiction, and we can trace the growth briefly in the three sections of *The Sun Also Rises*. There, the Hemingway hero suffers, first, the amoral chaos of the Paris cafes, then seeks to purge himself in the authentic life of the senses on a fishing trip, and, finally, commits himself to a code of conduct born in the ruthless skill of Romero, the bullfighter. Later, the code is to be found in the familiar Hemingway world of boxer, big-game hunter, or soldier of fortune; in Harry Morgan, the simple patriarch, or Santiago, the enduring fisherman.

It is, then, as though *A Farewell to Arms* suffers the "Nada who art in Nada" of the smoky wartime cafes, respects the moral achievement in the surgeon's code, but prefers to focus on the second stage, the mode of authentic perception, furnishing its rationale in the priest's image of Abruzzi, and dramatizing its career in Henry's dogged determination to achieve direct sensory knowledge of the inexhaustible surfaces of the world. For, despite the routine cliché of its subject, there is nothing throughout the novel but the sense of felt life, experience with whose radical concreteness there can be no quarrel.

Henry, then, is the Hero as Esthetician, a modern man who is finished getting embarrassed in churches, exhausted by wine and dialectic, frustrated by the exclusiveness of fishing trips, walks in Abruzzi, and the literally unpracticeable disciplines of his abandoned architectural studies. In the ultimate chaos of his time, in a world at war, he is simply not impressed, and refuses to abbreviate his awareness of what it feels like to make love, ride in a freight car, or dive into a river. He will always insist on knowing what the weather is like. And, though in steady danger of boring us with the copiousness of his detail, Hemingway has provided his hero with irony sufficient to discourage the reader's impatience.

It is inevitable that Hemingway will pay equal attention to the sweetness of Henry's wine, the texture of the sheets under which he makes love, and the temperature of the water in which he escapes to his separate peace. For the big words, the meaningful hierarchies of civilized value, can no longer account for his experience. The important thing is to stop the room from whirling, and, for Hemingway's purposes, concentrating on a wall or a flower, the side of a mountain, or a package of cigarettes is equally valid.

Erich Auerbach, in discussing the representation of reality in contemporary Western literature, has remarked on the modern writer's obsession with the simple fact, the random occurrence:

> What takes place . . . in works of this kind . . . is to put the emphasis on the random occurrence, to exploit it not in the service of a planned continuity of action but in itself, and in the process something new appears: nothing less than the wealth of reality and depth of life in every moment to which we surrender ourselves without prejudice. It is precisely the random moment which is comparatively independent of the controversial and unstable orders over which men fight and despair; it passes unaffected by them as daily life.

Auerbach, finally, is optimistic about the eventual recovery, through this technique, of more sophisticated systems of value:

> The more it [the random occurrence] is exploited, the more the elementary things which our lives have in common come to light. In this unprejudiced and exploratory type of representation we cannot but see to what extent—below the surface conflicts—the differences between men's way of life and forms of thought have already lessened. . . . It is still a long way to a common life of mankind on earth but the goal begins to be visible.

There is, however, a further complexity in the structure of Hemingway's novel. For precisely as the chaos of war clears in tension against the firm, precise, dense acts of perception, so the irony functions in another way. It complicates, through the rich, suggestive, sensory detail, the essentially pedestrian plot, the routine love story of wound, hospital, separate peace, pregnancy, and death in childbirth. The style of Henry's perception is employed as arbiter between the world's unsubduable nightmare and the simple, tedious daylight of the personal life, focusing the war while expanding the love story. . . .

In Hemingway's love story, the fresh concrete surfaces of the fragmentary experiences renew the sense of life possible even in the cemetery of war, while, simultaneously, the lovers' instinct to develop their relationship from sex to love to, finally, an eagerness at the prospect of a child, reflects the persistent human effort not alone to make sense of life, but to believe it as well, to recover at last, in Auerbach's phrase, "the common life of mankind on earth.". . .

In Hemingway's final irony, Catherine is destroyed, not by the war, but by the small hips that would have killed her in Minneapolis, by the same inscrutable fate that arranges for retreats at Caporetto, lovemaking in Milan, and, ultimately, the perennial resource of Abruzzi.

Hemingway's solution throughout *A Farewell to Arms* has been neither to succumb to the war's paralyzing morbidity nor to undertake to resist directly its violent catastrophe. It has been, rather, to focus on what is immediate and dense, and unequivocal and human in the narrator's experience of it. The novel's achievement is in its determination to exploit, if sometimes too painstakingly, the ground on which, if it is ever possible again, a meaningful vision of the human condition will have to be constructed. The style, in short, has been made the symbol.

# Food as an Element of the "Iceberg Principle"

Linda Underhill and Jeanne Nakjavani

Hemingway uses food in his writing as concrete, specific images that add impact and immediacy to his work and help establish him as a knowledgeable authority on the places he writes about. Writers Linda Underhill and Jeanne Nakjavani examine Hemingway's use of food and eating imagery as a code to signify the prevailing mood of characters and setting. This is in accord with Hemingway's "iceberg principle"—his theory that if the writer knew thoroughly what was going on with his characters, actions, and scenes, he only needed to show a few details (the visible, above-water portion of the iceberg) and the reader would understand the remainder (the vast majority of the berg, which is under water). The authors point out that he also uses food to provide what he called "true" information about foreign foods and manners.

More than any other American writer, Ernest Hemingway inspired the lifestyle of "living it up to write it down." He traveled the world, drove an ambulance in World War I, boxed, married four times, hunted big game in Africa and big fish in the Gulf Stream. In general, he sampled most of what life had to offer, including the food and drink of many nations. He conveyed his experiences through his memoirs and newspaper articles, many of which appeared in the *Toronto Star.* "As a reporter and correspondent," says William White, editor of the two published volumes of Hemingway's journalism, "Hemingway soaked up persons and places and life like a sponge; these were to become matter for his short stories and novels." As White points out, Hemingway simply transferred nonfiction accounts to fictitious

From Linda Underhill and Jeanne Nakjavani, "Food for Fiction: Lessons from Ernest Hemingway's Writing," *Journal of American Culture*, Summer 1992. Reprinted by permission of the Popular Culture Press.

narratives. It was this "voice of experience and much-traveled source of inside information," as Charles Scribner Jr. called it, which was responsible for his much imitated persona as well as the success of his fiction.

In his fictional accounts of food, he frequently drew upon his experience as a self-proclaimed gourmet to add the heightened awareness necessary to create a mood in critical scenes. The "romance" of food, as he called it, or the adventure of food, becomes, in Hemingway's novels, a way of heightening the mood of a scene whenever the characters themselves are in for an adventure. There are times in Hemingway's fiction when meals are simply meals, and at these times Hemingway gives no details regarding food. In moments of intense excitement or danger, however, every detail is important. The way people eat and *what they eat* at these points of crisis suggest the heightened emotional state of the characters in the scene. At these times, food becomes a code which signifies the prevailing mood of the adventure. This aided Hemingway in his "iceberg principle" style, which leaves much of the significance beneath the surface.

Another function of food is by providing accurate, or what Hemingway would call "true," information about foreign foods, Hemingway gives expatriate characters status as citizens of the world. By eating the foods the natives eat, often even sharing the same bowl, bottle, or plate with them, the expatriate heroes take sustenance to strengthen themselves for an adventure in a foreign land and absorb the native culture through the food, taking part in the culture so as to experience the adventure truly, as a native would. As Hemingway himself told his sister Marcelline, "Don't be afraid to taste all the other things in life that aren't in Oak Park. This life is all right, but there's a whole big world out there."

## EARLY INFLUENCE

Food was in fact an important aspect of life to the Hemingway family. Ernest Hemingway's father, Dr. Clarence Hemingway, took a great interest in food, nutrition, and cooking, and provided his son with an early influence for thinking of food as adventure. According to Marcelline, in her book *At the Hemingways*, Dr. Hemingway kept "a good supply of food on hand," and encouraged the Hemingway children to try all sorts of unusual foods. She says Dr. Hemingway "liked initiative in us, whether in trying a new recipe or starting on some other idea." He made the children try new foods at least four times, his theory being that one could educate the taste buds by eating something four times. . . .

Dr. Hemingway also encouraged his children to hunt, and taught them all to shoot and fish. However, they were instructed never to shoot more than they could eat. Marcelline tells a hilarious story about Ernest and his friend Harold Sampson shooting a porcupine once for fun at their summer home on Walloon Lake, Michigan. When Dr. Hemingway learned of their escapades, he demanded they cook the animal and eat it. Sampson wrote Marcelline that "we cooked the haunches for hours but they were still about as tender and tasty as a piece of shoe leather. We never killed another porcupine." Marcelline quotes her father's philosophy: "It takes judgement to shoot. It takes kindness to kill cleanly, and it takes a wise man never to shoot more than he can use to eat."

By the time he was an adult, Hemingway had clearly learned to associate food with adventure. In a 1923 article for the *Toronto Star Weekly*, he details his "gastronomic adventures," saying, at the age of 24:

> I have eaten Chinese sea slugs, muskrat, porcupine, beaver tails, birds' nests, octopus and horse meat. I have also eaten snails, eels, sparrows, caviar and spaghetti. All shapes. In addition I have at one time or another eaten Chinese river shrimps, bamboo sprouts, hundred-year-old eggs, and lunch-counter doughnuts. Finally I must confess to having eaten mule meat, bear meat, moose meat, frogs legs, and fritto misto.

He concludes, "I have discovered that there is romance in food when romance has disappeared from everywhere else. And as long as my digestion holds out I will follow romance."

## FOOD INDICATES MOOD

Hemingway's pledge to the "romance," or adventure, of food could be taken lightly if it were not for the innumerable descriptions of food and drink in his fiction. Unlike many other writers to whom food is a curious aspect of the background detail, a way of describing a character's tastes, or an indicator of some other social or political aspect of the story, in Hemingway's fiction food often provides a significant indicator for mood instead. When food is described in detail, it suggests the mood of a particular adventure. Game foods or fish are frequently included on the menu of these special meals to build excitement by association with the hunt.

In Hemingway's first novel, *The Sun Also Rises*, meals suggest the festive mood of the adventure in Pamplona, where the Spanish "World Series" of bullfights is held. Eating and drinking are part of the shared activities of the crowd at the fiesta of San Fermin, and Hemingway mentions in particular the famous Spanish tapas, appetizers served in the evening to stave off hunger while waiting for the very late Spanish dinner hour. He chooses to describe in particular a salad of fresh tuna, a fish not easy to catch.

---

### CHRISTMAS IN PARIS

It is very beautiful in Paris and very lonely at Christmas-time.

The young man and his girl walk up the Rue Bonaparte from the Quai in the shadow of the tall houses to the brightly lighted little Rue Jacob. In a little second-floor restaurant, The Veritable Restaurant of the Third Republic, which has two rooms, four tiny tables and a cat, there is a special Christmas dinner being served.

"It isn't much like Christmas," said the girl.

"I miss the cranberries," said the young man.

They attack the special Christmas dinner. The turkey is cut into a peculiar sort of geometrical formation that seems to include a small taste of meat, a great deal of gristle, and a large piece of bone.

"Do you remember turkey at home?" asks the young girl.

"Don't talk about it," says the boy.

They attack the potatoes, which are fried with too much grease.

"What do you suppose they're doing at home?" says the girl.

"I don't know," said the boy. "Do you suppose we'll ever get home?"...

The proprietor entered with the dessert and a small bottle of red wine.

"I had forgotten the wine," he said in French.

The girl began to cry.

"I didn't know Paris was like this," she said. "I thought it was gay and full of light and beautiful."...

You do not know what Christmas is until you lose it in some foreign land.

Ernest Hemingway, "Christmas on the Roof of the World," *Toronto Star Weekly*, December 22, 1923.

The evening the fiesta begins, or, as Hemingway says, "explodes," Jake Barnes goes to a wine shop to fill a leather wine-skin and finds Brett and his other companions "sitting on barrels surrounded by the dancers" in the back room, having an appetizer of fresh tuna salad. He says that Mike is "eating from a bowl of tuna fish, chopped onions and vinegar. They were all drinking wine and mopping up the oil and vinegar with pieces of bread." The Spaniards insist on sending for another fork, and all, including the Americans, eat from the same bowl. Barnes reciprocates by sharing wine from the wine-skin he has just purchased. Barnes and his companions are thus embraced by the native culture and share truly in the adventures Pamplona has to offer. Furthermore, the tuna, which in *By-Line* Hemingway calls "the king of fish," has "the ferocity of a mammoth rainbow trout." The excitement of landing one is a "purifying" experience, one equal to the victories in battle which would qualify one for entering the Valhalla. With such credentials, it is certainly a fish worthy of the role of appetizer at the bullfights, another dangerous and exciting adventure.

In contrast to the festive atmosphere of *The Sun Also Rises*, in Hemingway's second novel, *A Farewell to Arms*, the meals are a series of "last suppers" presaging an adventure of a far different kind. With the novel's opening, the Italian soldiers are in retreat, and they eat their meal at the mess like men on the run:

> Looking out at the snow falling slowly and heavily, we knew it was all over for that year. . . . Every one ate very quickly and seriously, lifting the spaghetti on the fork until the loose strands hung clear then lowering it into the mouth, or else using a continuous lift and sucking into the mouth, helping ourselves to wine from the grass-covered gallon flask.

This meal, eaten "quickly and seriously," reinforces the mood of retreat. There is nothing special about the spaghetti; the soldiers do not have time for enjoying their food, or even for forking it up properly, but just "shove it in." This food is merely sustenance and they are merely surviving. It is clear they are in danger.

Just before being wounded, Frederic Henry tries to get food for the disillusioned ambulance mechanics at the front. Only some leftover cheese and cold spaghetti are available, but the mechanics are hungry and Henry feels it is important they eat. He braves the shelling as he runs across the old brick yard to take the mechanics the food and arrives in the trench "holding the cheese, its smooth surface covered with brick dust." "I took out my knife," he goes on, "opened it, wiped off the blade and pared off the dirty outside surface of the cheese. Gavuzzi handed me the basin of macaroni." They eat the spaghetti from the bowl on the floor with their fingers, chewing the hard, cold macaroni and washing it down with wine which Henry says "tasted of rusty metal."

This meal is like the first in its haste but its details are even more desperate, prefiguring the shelling which will, in a few short moments, kill one of them and wound Henry. The food is ordinary, and worse yet, it is cold, dirty, and already tasting of the shells. The fact that Henry has food in his stomach when he is wounded makes his pain during the operation of his leg later much worse.

## FOOD AND LOVE

Paralleling these meals of retreat, Catherine Barkley and Frederic Henry have a special meal together in a hotel room attempting to satisfy their hunger for each other on the last day of Henry's stay in Milan. Hemingway says they are very hungry, and Catherine of course by this time is eating for two. The waiter at the hotel guesses their intentions and asks, "You wish something special for dinner. Some game or a soufflé?" Henry asks, "What have you as game?" When the waiter responds that he can get pheasant, or a woodcock, Henry chooses woodcock: "We were very hungry and the meal was good. . . . For dinner we had a woodcock with soufflé potatoes and purée de marron, a salad, and zabaione for dessert."

This very special meal of fine European delicacies made of fresh, "natural" foods like the game birds, chestnuts (marron), and potatoes, is intended to create a mood of "natural" happiness for the lovers. It works, if briefly. After the meal, Henry says that "we felt very fine, and then after, we felt very happy and in a little time the room felt like our home." Their happiness is fleeting, however, and the "special" meal becomes ironic, just as Catherine is ironic about their love making when she says she feels like a whore, and that the room looks like a bordello. They are hungry again soon afterward, when the time comes for Henry to leave for the front.

Henry's last supper comes just before Catherine's death at the end of the novel. He eats breakfast, lunch, and supper at a cafe down the street from the hospital where Catherine is in labor to deliver their son. At all three meals, the food is not enjoyable, but it is *described in detail.* For all three meals, there is only leftover food. Leaving the cafe after breakfast, Henry sees a dog nosing in the restaurant's garbage searching for food. There are only "coffee-grounds, dust, and some dead flowers," which can suggest a grave. Henry looks in vain for something to give the dog, but says, "There isn't anything." For lunch he has a sausage which he describes as "buried" in "hot wine-soaked cabbage," and it is following this meal that Henry learns the baby is delivered, dead. He is very concerned about Catherine, but the attending nurse urges him to go out and eat. At supper, Henry says, "It was hot in the cafe and the air was bad." The other customers are unfriendly. Henry eats and drinks, trying to calm himself, but suddenly has a premonition that Catherine needs him. He quickly returns to the hospital to find her dying. The imagery of these final meals is clearly associated with the last tragic adventure of Catherine's death from hemorrhage after a Caesarian, and indicates a mood of loss and grief. Although some readers find Henry's eating while Catherine is in labor to be a sign of callousness, it is important to recognize that he is urged to leave the hospital by both the staff and Catherine herself, who says, at the beginning of her labor, "You go away, darling. . . . Go out and get something to eat. I may do this for a long time."

## FOOD AND DANGER

In his next novel, Hemingway's hero Robert Jordan shares an important meal with the Spanish peasants in an early scene from *For Whom the Bell Tolls.* Just arrived at the cave where they are hiding, Jordan has been talking about the dangers of their plan to dynamite a bridge with Pablo and the gypsy, drinking their wine and sharing his tobacco with them. They question whether Jordan would want to be shot if he were wounded as had been his predecessor Kashkin, the Russian, and he says, "Listen to me clearly. If ever I should have any little favors to ask of any man, I will ask him at the time." The gypsy approves. "In this way speak the good ones," he says.

Just as this sign of approval is given, Maria, who will become Jordan's lover, brings out an iron platter of rabbit stew, "cooked with onions and green peppers and . . . chick peas in the red wine sauce." She puts forks against the iron platter and they all eat "out of the platter, not speaking, as is the Spanish custom." Thus Jordan is initiated into the customs of the group, drinking their wine, eating authentic peasant food, sharing in their struggle, and at the same time falling in love with the woman who has served it.

While this meal also includes game, it is special not so much because of the ingredients, which are plentiful—rabbit being available when there is nothing else to hunt—but because it represents the desperation of the resistance and their need for sustenance in the wilderness as they embark on a dangerous adventure. Jordan thinks the stew is "delicious," mopping up every drop of sauce, just as he joins in their struggle with no qualifications. Later in the story, the same stew is served again, only this time with wild mushrooms foraged from the forest instead of the chick peas, showing the peasants to be even more desperate. At this point they have to be urged to eat by Jordan and Maria, having lost their appetite for the war.

Jake Barnes, Frederic Henry, and Robert Jordan are all examples of Hemingway's expatriate heroes having adventures in a foreign country. Hemingway avoids cultural stereotypes and lends "truth" to these characters' adventures by including very accurate, specific details about foreign food and drink, those which would probably only be fully appreciated by food "aficionados." He disdained uninformed tourists, calling them "scum" and comparing them to the taste of "a jug of soured molasses" in the *Toronto Star Weekly*. Tourists always paid too much and fell for the phony entertainments created for them by the locals. Hemingway wanted his fictional expatriate heroes to be more than tourists, to know "the truth" about foreign food and drink, and to have true adventures. Therefore, in *The Sun Also Rises*, Jake Barnes orders "Jerez" rather than any other type of sherry just as the fiesta begins, because Hemingway knew it was considered the only true Spanish sherry. If you know a thing, as Hemingway says, you can leave it out. Tuna, the "king of fish," is no accident as an appetizer; it has the most value as an adventure for the fisherman. Frederic Henry chooses woodcock over pheasant for his special supper with Catherine because he knows as did Hemingway that it is the rarer and considered a great delicacy by the hunter.

Hemingway also knew that along with the chestnuts and potatoes, the woodcock would have been at the prime of its delicacy in the autumn, when this meal is served. In a 1935 article on hunting for *Esquire,* he exclaimed, "What a bird to eat flambé with armagnac cooked in his own juice and butter, a little mustard added to make a sauce, with two strips of bacon and pommes soufflé." The soufflé potatoes and chestnut purée, a traditional accompaniment to game, compliment the woodcock in a way that a gourmet cook would appreciate to make a romantic meal for the Hemingway lovers.

Hemingway recalls his pleasure on tasting these dishes, as well as the jugged hare stew from *For Whom the Bell Tolls,* in his memoir, *A Moveable Feast,* and in his *Esquire* article quoted previously. His favorite Spanish wine and tapas are mentioned by Mary Hemingway in her memoir *How it Was,* and by Jose Luis Castillo-Puche in his book *Hemingway in Spain,* among others.

As a result of this kind of specific detail, food and drink in Hemingway's fiction become, at moments of crisis in the story, a code to signify the mood, lending truth to the setting, and representing adventure.

# Conrad's Influence on Hemingway

Jeffrey Meyers

Hemingway acknowledged his appreciation of and debt to author Joseph Conrad, writes Hemingway biographer Jeffrey Meyers. Among the influences that can be attributed to Conrad are the heroic code of honor, stoicism, the need to test oneself in extreme situations, and finding and trying to communicate the "truth" of one's own sensations.

A thorough study of Joseph Conrad's influence [on modern writers] would require a whole book. . . .

Conrad's influence was particularly powerful on . . . Ernest Hemingway. In 1923, while working as a reporter on the Toronto *Daily Star*, Hemingway went up to Sudbury, north of Lake Huron in Canada, to expose a fake coal company and consoled himself by reading *The Rover* in the Nickel Range Hotel. "When morning came I had used up all my Conrad like a drunkard," Hemingway wrote, describing himself as Conrad's literary heir. "I had hoped it would last me the trip, and felt like a young man who has blown in his patrimony."

The following year, back in Paris, Hemingway contributed to the "Conrad Supplement" of Ford Madox Ford's *Transatlantic Review*, which appeared shortly after Conrad's death. The young Hemingway, just beginning his literary career, paid tribute to the novelist by favorably comparing him (in his worst jocular style) to [T.S.] Eliot, who had recently published *The Waste Land*, and by acknowledging the lesson of the master: "If I knew that by grinding Mr. Eliot into a fine dry powder and sprinkling that powder over Mr. Conrad's grave Mr. Conrad would shortly appear, looking very annoyed at the forced return, and commence writing, I would leave for London early tomorrow morning with a sausage

From Jeffrey Meyers, "Conrad's Influence on Modern Writers," *Twentieth Century Literature*, Summer 1990.

grinder." Hemingway concluded by affirming: "From nothing else that I have ever read have I gotten what every book of Conrad has given me."

## ECHOES OF CONRAD

Conrad's emphasis on stoicism, on a heroic ethos and a code of honor, and on testing oneself in violent and extreme situations, profoundly affected Hemingway. In *The Sun Also Rises* (1926) he adopts Stein's phrase about Lord Jim, "one of us," to characterize Count Mippipopolous, who had been wounded by arrows in Abyssinia. And the description of Ricardo carefully shaving before meeting Lena in *Victory* may have influenced "all that barbering" that Robert Cohn does to prepare himself for Brett Ashley. In *A Farewell to Arms* (1929) Catherine Barkley is as completely self-effacing as Lena, who tells Heyst: "If you were to stop thinking of me I shouldn't be in the world at all!... I can only be what you think I am." "The Short Happy Life of Francis Macomber" (1936) re-creates the great Conradian theme of moral failure and recovery of self-esteem just as *The Old Man and the Sea* (1952) portrays Conrad's theme of victory in defeat.

---

### JOSEPH CONRAD ON HIS HERO NOSTROMO

In his firm grip on the earth he inherits, in his improvidence and generosity, in his lavishness with his gifts, in his manly vanity, in the obscure sense of his greatness, and in his faithful devotion with something despairing as well as desperate in its impulses, he is a Man of the People, their very own unenvious force.... In his mingled love and scorn of life and in the bewildered conviction of having been betrayed, of dying betrayed he hardly knows by what or by whom, he is still of the People, their undoubted Great Man —with a private history of his own.

Joseph Conrad, "Author's Note," *Nostromo*, 1904.

---

Conrad's belief in "scrupulous fidelity to the truth of my own sensations," expressed in his Author's Note to *Within the Tides*, is echoed in Hemingway's desire to portray "the actual things which produced the emotion that you experienced." The most important lesson came from Conrad's aesthetic pronouncement, the Preface to *The Nigger of the "Narcissus,"* which stressed the visual element in fiction: "My task which I am trying to achieve is, by the power of the written word to make you hear, to make you feel—it is, before all, to make you see." Hemingway repeated this artistic credo when he insisted that the novelist must "find what gave you the emotion; what the action was that gave you the excitement. Then write it down making it clear so the reader will see it too."

A description of a Mediterranean landscape from *The Rover*—which resembles a cinematic tracking-shot that moves from the sky and the mountains to the trees on the plain and the red-tiled roofs of the farmhouses—shows quite precisely how Hemingway learned from and imitated Conrad in *The Sun Also Rises:*

> There were leaning pines on the skyline, and in the pass itself dull silvery green patches of olive orchards below a long yellow wall backed by dark cypresses, and the red roofs of buildings which seemed to belong to a farm. [*The Rover*]

> [The mountains] were wooded and there were clouds coming down from them. The green plain stretched off. It was cut by fences and the white of the road showed through the trunks of a double line of trees that crossed the plain toward the north. As we came to the edge of the rise we saw the red roofs and the white houses of Burguete ahead strung out on the plain. [*The Sun Also Rises*]

Later on, the older Hemingway was more severe on Conrad's character. In February 1944 Hemingway, distracted by the war, criticized Conrad's self-pity and complaints (following the agonized tradition of Flaubert) in a letter to his editor, Max Perkins: "I miss writing very much Max. You see, unlike the people who belabored it as a dog's life *ce métier de chien* Conrad and old Ford were always suffering about. I loved to write very much and was never happier than doing it.". . .

[But] Conrad's code of behavior, moral strength, and his ability to create a "heroic country of the soul" [are] confirmed by Jan Szczepanski, who poignantly observes in "The Conrad of My Generation" (1957): "His books became a collection of practical recipes for men fighting lonely battles in the dark."

# The Universe on Edge

David Hughes

Using the simplest words, Hemingway achieved effects of high subtlety in his writing, declares David Hughes, editor of a British edition of Hemingway stories. Hughes points out that the early short stories maintain an intensity that reflected their author's own experiences. The Nick Adams stories, though separate, hang together and provide a kind of alter ego for the author. Through Nick, Hemingway presents his vision of twentieth-century anguish. With fame and luxury he lost the honesty of the Nick stories; as he became a public person, he began to avoid the hard work of perceiving and writing with such concentration. Although his novels are grander in scale, they lack the intensity of his short stories.

It is hard to write about Hemingway without thinking like Hemingway. He is very infectious. When you read him your mind begins to work in his rhythms and to throw out all the adverbs and to cut out every verbal flourish in favour of plain pictorial narrative that states its own case. But he is also inimitable. No writer ever worked harder to keep himself out of his stories, yet no style bears more of the stamp of its author. His ability to use so few words and such curt ones to convey matters of life and death was the result of a long struggle to banish the literary from his language.

So Hemingway's art has a very small 'a' and is buried as deep as the message. He left so much unsaid in his stories that they say far more than you think. They work on emotion. 'If the writer of prose knows enough about what he is writing about he may omit things that he knows, and the reader, if the writer is writing truly enough, will have a feeling of those things as strongly as though the writer had stated them.'. . . His stories were made to be as incontrovertible as fact, to speak uniquely for themselves. He was as

From the Introduction by David Hughes to *Short Stories* by Ernest Hemingway (London: Folio Society, 1986). Copyright 1986 by The Folio Society Ltd. Reproduced by permission of The Folio Society Ltd.

hard on fakes as he was on wordsmiths. 'No matter how good a phrase or a simile he may have, if he puts it in where it is not absolutely necessary and irreplaceable he is spoiling his work for egotism.'. . .

Foremost there was the prose. To give the right weight to each word, his habit was to  put  two  or  three  times more  space  than  usual  between  them when typing a story out. These words he found all the harder to choose for being easy ones. What he had to say wasn't that simple, but had to look it. Did Faulkner really think big emotions came from big words? 'He thinks I don't know the ten-dollar words,' Hemingway said. 'I know them all right. But there are older and simpler and better words, and those are the ones I use'—they were words which Edmund Wilson less simply described as strings of Nordic monosyllables, declarative sentences, colloquial American speech. Out of such words, out of what unliterary hunters or illiterate bullfighters uttered when they unknowingly meant more than they said, Hemingway dug effects of high subtlety. He decided that his task, in descriptions that were cut to the bone, was to reveal all about a place by concealing his view of it. Mostly it was dialogue that bore the weight of feeling. Ford Madox Ford—a friend who like many others was taken up by Hemingway for his uses, then dropped for his failures—hit upon the metaphor for this pared style: 'His words strike you, each one, as if they were pebbles fetched fresh from a brook. They live and shine, each in its place.' Hemingway himself could hardly have used shorter words, more succinctly.

Then there was the content. Already, at twenty-three, Hemingway had faced up to most of the material he would use. All of it expressed or symbolised the special violence of this century. It sprang from war at first hand, from avalanches and bullrings and marriages; but mostly from his American childhood, that clash of city and wilderness, which had opened up in him such a sensitivity to pain and a determination to crack down on the human condition and, in his own now hackneyed phrase, show it the way it was. He loved the way it was; he hated it for not being better. No author ever put up a cockier fight against what he saw as our melancholy pause between womb and grave and none has so frankly relished more of its pleasures. Without falsity he viewed the business of living as a sport against 'that old whore' death, in playing which a man could die but not be defeated, and it was natural that most of the stories had sportsmen as central figures, their very inarticulacy a conduit of raw feeling.

## NICK ADAMS, ALTER EGO

Nearly every story has a Hemingway type in it, battling with courage against hideous odds. But for many of the best ones, to lend perspective to his definitive vision of twentieth-century anguish, he invented an alter ego called Nicholas Adams. In early stories like 'Indian Camp' he is a small boy compelled by circumstances to witness a childbirth so agonising that the father slits his own throat. The shock is underplayed, like all the most ghastly of Hemingway's events. Thereafter, in subsequent stories, Nick is to grow up hard and fast. Soon we find him, with his father or a young chum, colluding against women, despairing of their humanity. Then an international war rubs off yet more of his innocence, reducing his hopes of life, deepening his misery of spirit even as it prompts him to the exercise of manly virtues. Then the war is over and he is scarred perhaps for good, wondering how to digest the effects of conflict and turn them to positive use, yet hating in his guts the tedium of peace. He identifies with the loneliness of matadors in their seedy lodgings and sees his own struggle reflected in their brushes with death.

Through all these experiences Nick is neurosis personified; the very universe is on edge. To calm down on his return from Europe he pits his wits against trout in the rivers or game in the forests. The emptiness of wild country succours but challenges him: there is no rest for a character as fragmented, as inwardly hurt but apparently normal, as Nick Adams. Hemingway deliberately keeps him very much like us—or at least the way we see ourselves—fearful, changeable, hard to get to know—yet reading these stories, as he jumps the gap from one obliquely significant event to the next, we feel him growing and breaking out of the limits of himself and becoming a man of his time and thus telling us between the lines how to live. The stories in which Nick appears, though quite separate, hang together. They share the same emotional voice, tight-lipped, hiding pain, spare with humour. If you put them in rough sequence, they fashion a biography of the spirit that is hard to equal as an account of one man's resilience in the grip of despair. No writer has ever caught at such speed what calls in the reader for a good deal of slow thought.

Thus linked the stories show in an orderly way how Nick Adams comes to terms with the disorder of our century. It would be artificial to claim that this editorial device achieves a hidden self-portrait of the author. Hemingway, with his belief in the autocracy of fiction, would have denied to the last that stories he meant to be realistic but also surreal corresponded in so direct a manner with the reality of his life. Nick Adams is only to some extent an idealised projection of his creator. The stories are only to some extent a series of sketches for the faintly exaggerated and more than slightly preposterous Hemingway hero who struck attitudes in the novels. But, more touchingly than all that, they do make up a picture of the inner man with all his complications, set out in the simplest terms but also highly sidelong, quite a bit oblique.

## STRETCHING STORIES INTO NOVELS

Somehow the novel seems to me to be an awfully artificial and worked out form but as some of the short stories now are stretching out to 8000 to 12000 words maybe I'll get there yet.

Ernest Hemingway, in Carlos Baker, ed., *Ernest Hemingway, Selected Letters 1917–61*, 1981.

When he wrote these stories Hemingway was being honest. As soon as fame came his way in the thirties and luxury loomed, playing hard, drinking harder, working less hard, fighting lions in the bush or marlins in the ocean or the women in his life, Hemingway fell into his own trap. He developed with depressing dash into what his sternest admirer, Edmund Wilson, called 'the false or publicity Hemingway,' pretending in public to kick against intrusions on his private life, but in fact embracing them because they let him off the hook of words. He could avoid the perceptions he had once hunted. He could go fishing instead of rising to more serious bait. Being as drunk on fame as on daiquiris seemed a lesser annoyance than soberly seeking out yet more truth. Perhaps there wasn't any more to be had. One of his later stories, 'The Snows of Kilimanjaro,' tells the tale of his treachery to himself, as he saw it. You died when there was no more to be said. . . .

## A FLAMBOYANT MINIATURIST

How should we read these stories now? It's worth recalling that Hemingway, though big and brawny and given to flamboyance, was a miniaturist. He once said that he never set out to write a novel, only a story which sometimes got longer. 'Let the pressure build,' he said. And the novels, though superficially easier to read, as grand in scale as the man himself, certainly miss the intensity of pressure which he managed to contain within many a story a few sides long. Edmund Wilson, incisively appreciating his American coevals—Sherwood Anderson, Scott Fitzgerald, Sinclair Lewis—who burst into a blaze of fiction between the wars, granted a lesser place in the canon for Hemingway's novels. 'The people in his short stories are satisfactory', he wrote, 'because he has only to hit them off: the point of the story does not lie in personalities, but in the emotion to which a situation gives rise.'

This, added to Hemingway's gift for always tackling vital issues while hardly dwelling on them—marriage, death, abortion, adolescence, war, divorce, to name only the least happy—keeps his short work more vigorous, and deeper, and less of a cartoon of the man that he was or the time when he wrote. He must have guessed in youth that his life was doomed by his own strong-armed standards to unhappiness and failure, for his power was to convey disquiet, to grate on our inner nerves, to convince us that we live in an age of hopeless malaise, which we have no choice but to face with grit, regard with pity, fight with honour—and end by understanding. But there is always hope and light too. He raises qualms in us, only to catalyse them, to counterbalance them with a delight in earthly pleasures, and he brings that irony to us time and again with an economy of means unmatched in prose. 'The great thing,' he said in the final sentences of *Death in the Afternoon*, 'is to last and get your work done and see and hear and learn and understand; and write when there is something that you know; and not before; and not too damned much after . . .' He lived up to that.

Anyway I love this man's work, so let's end with an anecdote that shows the endearing old monster at his best, an ironist of iron will who was kindly to strangers even after the swelling of his ego had misled him into taking fame more seriously than words. He knew that many people felt, and will still feel, that there's no point to his stories; even he could hardly dispense with a beginning, but the middle often seems muddled and there's no apparent end—he just stops. Perhaps he figured that a piece he had written so many times, just to give it beauty or to make it perfect, was entitled to no less effort from the reader, who might have to read it just as many times to plumb it. So he somewhere records once telling an old lady a story that just tailed off, as so many of them do at first acquaintance. 'Is there not to be', she asked, 'what we called in my youth a wow at the end?'

'Ah, Madame,' Hemingway replied, 'it is years since I added the wow to the end of the story'—and he gently spelt out the point for her.

'This seems to me a very feeble wow,' she said.

'Madame'—and you can hear his patience, his courtesy, his total belief in the value of his tale, his knowledge of his own originality, his naive desire to be liked—'Madame,' he said, 'the whole subject is feeble and too hearty a wow would overbalance it.'

A nice modest note to end on, except that his subjects are never feeble. And the balance is exquisite. And the wow is hidden.

# CHAPTER 4

# Hemingway Reconsidered

# An Ongoing Revaluation of Hemingway

Keith Ferrell

After Hemingway's suicide, critics quickly began re-considering his place in the rank of American authors. Changing academic styles and social concerns led to a critical devaluation of his works for a couple of decades, but readers ignored the critics and continued to admire his achievements. Posthumous publication of some works left unfinished at the time of his death, collections of stories and journalistic work, and a large volume of his correspondence have offered a wider look at his skills and personality, and his reputation is once again on the rise.

That Hemingway's death would be a major news story was, of course, already known. Among his estate a collection of yellowing obituaries offered prescient testimony to the celebrity value of Hemingway dead. This time the obituaries were accurate, and his suicide made headlines worldwide.

At first, the death was reported as an accident, but the truth soon surfaced. Suicide gave those who had for years fashioned careers out of speculations on Ernest Hemingway's psychology an entirely new field to work. Could they find the seeds of his suicide in the pages of his books? Second-guessing Hemingway's suicide became virtually a small industry unto itself, with theories and explanations for the suicide filling newspaper columns, magazine articles, and, later, entire books. The theories proved as various as their authors, but proved little. An explanation might best be obtained by paraphrasing Hemingway himself: he died, and then he was dead.

The work he had done during his lifetime remained alive, however, and as the gossip columnists and pseudo-psychologists wrestled with his corpse, the critics—Hemingway's old nemeses—wrestled with his literary corpus. What was Hemingway's position in American literature? Was he, as he had so often proclaimed, the best, the champion? Such questions are finally unanswerable, but a full-scale critical revision got quickly under way. During the 1960s and 1970s, the academic and literary communities relegated Ernest Hemingway and his work to lower and lower status. If they could not make a convincing case for labeling him a minor writer, many critics argued that he at least had not been a major writer.

Despite the prizes he'd been awarded, despite Hemingway's enormous popularity and the phenomenal success of *The Old Man and the Sea*, the critical consensus after Hemingway's death was that he had ultimately failed as an artist. Hemingway's work as a stylist had certainly exercised a revolution in prose, but he had never delivered the ambitious novel many expected. *For Whom the Bell Tolls* fell from favor, coming to be seen as a fantasy romance of heroism and doomed love. *To Have and Have Not* and *Across the River and into the Trees* were declared to be minor works, and flawed minor works at that. Even *The Old Man and the Sea* failed fully to survive the new critical scrutiny: the book was too simple, some critics said; it lacked the complexity necessary for an important work. Hemingway's nonfiction, the journalism and *Death in the Afternoon* and *Green Hills of Africa*, were viewed as interesting only in the ways in which they shed light on Ernest Hemingway's character and obsessions.

There was important work among Hemingway's books: *The Sun Also Rises*, *A Farewell to Arms*, and many of the short stories retained their power and beauty, the critical line went. But, the line went on, wasn't that really a rather small achievement? Certainly Hemingway had not left an artistic record on the order of that of William Faulkner, his old rival. Even Scott Fitzgerald, whose work at one time had been out of print, received a more admiring critical press during the 1960s and 1970s than did Ernest Hemingway.

How could Hemingway have fallen from grace so quickly? In part his decline can be seen as a measure of the times during which the revision occurred. The virtues Hemingway extolled in his work—courage, masculinity, grace under fire—seemed out of place to many in the 1960s. Bravery was old-fashioned, courage an anachronism in the shadow of nuclear weapons. What place could grace hold on a battlefield whose combatants were missiles, not men? War, in Hemingway's life and art the great consolidating experience, became the object of protest, soldiers the object of scorn.

As the women's movement gathered strength during the decades after Hemingway's death, his hairy-chested mas-culinity was denounced as foolish and even dangerous. Feminist writers attacked Hemingway's work with some fre-quency. Racist and anti-Semitic strains were found and de-nounced in his work. Even the hunting and fishing expedi-tions, so long seen as tests of courage and celebrations of the adventurous life, were now condemned as cruel, even per-verse. Thanks to Hemingway and others like him, it was ar-gued, many noble species came to be balanced on the edge of extinction.

### So Unseemly

When Ernest Hemingway died, there were copious obitu-ary notices; it was front page news. However, the obituaries were those of a public image, more than of a writer. Even his death was publicity. Anecdotes played more of a role in commemorating him than did accomplishments. How he fished and fought was more newsworthy than significant events in his career as a writer. He was praised for having "cooled" some night club characters who were left un-named. The fracas with Max Eastman in which Ernest did not come out so well was revised so as to help make Ernest a slugging hero. The simple declarative sentences which he often used were treated by another obituary writer as a major innovation in literary style. It was all unseemly.

James T. Farrell, "Ernest Hemingway," *Fitzgerald/Hemingway Annual*, 1973.

But there is the critical community, and there is the read-ing public. Ernest Hemingway's work fell into academic dis-repute, but readers never lost their admiration for Heming-way's achievement. His concerns—courage, dignity, clarity of thought and expression—proved themselves universal; the manifestations of his personality had interest without damaging the value of the work. Hemingway's books re-mained in print and sold well in hard and soft covers; films made of the books and stories attracted audiences; works unpublished at his death found eager readers when they came to be published.

Mary Hemingway proved herself an able and careful

manager of her husband's literary estate. There was no rush to get Hemingway's unpublished works into print. The first of the books to be published posthumously was the collection of sketches of Paris and Hemingway's youth, which in 1964 was brought out by Scribners as *A Moveable Feast.* It received generally respectful reviews, although the cruelty that colored many of Hemingway's portraits bothered some.

In 1970 Mary Hemingway chose to publish one of Hemingway's novels. This was the large sea story on which he had worked, under several titles, at various times during the last fifteen years of his life. The story of Thomas Hudson, artist—a not heavily disguised portrait of Hemingway himself—was published by Scribners as *Islands in the Stream.* The novel made the best-seller lists immediately and, though flawed, earned respectable reviews. Hemingway had not considered the book finished, but, except for some unspecified cuts in the manuscript, the book was published as written. The last section of *Islands in the Stream* told the story of Hudson's use of his fishing boat in pursuit of Nazis, and was an exciting if somewhat confused and incredible adventure story. The first section of the book, though, dealt with Hudson's life in Bimini and the long summer visit of his three sons, and was a fine, moving, and in places very funny novella.

Two years later, Scribners collected the Nick Adams stories and added a good number of unpublished fragments about Nick, one of them, of some length, perhaps the beginning of a novel. *The Nick Adams Stories* put the stories for the first time into chronological order, but the arrangement did little to increase the stories' already high stature. The fragments were interesting, although generally undistinguished, and the book was not a great success with the critics or the public.

*The Wild Years,* published in 1962, and *By-Line: Ernest Hemingway,* which appeared in 1967, collected Hemingway's newspaper and magazine journalism. In the case of these two volumes, chronological order became a genuine contribution, making Hemingway's skills, limitations, and growth as a journalist, a writer, and a celebrity evident....

Although Ernest Hemingway maintained that he did not wish his correspondence ever to be published—and made a sort of legal provision against such publication—Mary Hemingway bravely and wisely countermanded his instructions and in 1981 brought out *Ernest Hemingway: Selected Letters,*

*1917–1961.* The book is nearly one thousand pages long and was assembled under the editorship of Dr. Carlos Baker, the best of Hemingway's many biographers. The letters are pure Hemingway: loud, brash, compassionate, learned, funny, obscene, insecure, provocative, contemptuous. It is good to have the letters in print, and reading them brings their author to life as fully as can a biography.

Hemingway's name remains in the public eye in other ways than through his books. Bumby—now known as Jack—frequently appears on television wielding a fly rod, catching—and releasing—large trout. His granddaughters are even more famous. Margaux is a model and actress, and Mariel Hemingway is an actress who seems likely to become a major motion picture star. Both women are striking, with broad, familiar Hemingway grins.

As the century moves toward its close, Hemingway's position is becoming more secure, his reputation once more on the rise. Ernest Hemingway worried about such things, but need not have been too much concerned finally with his popular recognition. A quarter of a century after his death, the name *Ernest Hemingway* remains in many minds synonymous with "American writer," and his influence on younger writers continues undiminished. It is interesting, if empty, to speculate upon what he would have made of this modern world of computers, ambisexuality, television, movie stars who were his granddaughters, biological engineering, space travel. Interesting but empty, because with his death Hemingway dealt himself out of confrontation with a world in transition. He had seen enough transitions in his lifetime, and he left his life only after capturing, in works that may live forever, his reactions to those changes, his life and his attitudes, his fears and bravery, and the fears and attitudes and lives of another, now gone, age.

# The Sun Also Rises, Sixty Years Later

John W. Aldridge

The volume of information available about Hemingway and his work makes it difficult to read his writing with a fresh eye, admits literary essayist John W.
Aldridge in this 1986 appraisal of the author's first
novel. Yet, he says, sixty years after the publication of
*The Sun Also Rises*, the book still stands as a significant work of literature. Hemingway's powerful response to experience and a tight minimalist style
were the tools he used to create a morally fastidious
world. His complex artistry allows a glimpse of fearful and tragic adventure, concealed in shadow, and
his characters demonstrate a lesson in heroism as
they face the nihilism that threatens to engulf them.

Since 1961, the sheer volume of critical and biographical information about Hemingway has reached the proportions of
a corporate industry, with branches and subsidiaries
spreading across the world into virtually every civilized
country where his work has been translated and published.
The immediate result has been to inflate still further the already overblown Hemingway legend and to elevate almost
everything he wrote, both the best and the worst, to the status of holy scripture, while he himself is securely established as the imperial icon of American literature in the first
half of the twentieth century.

The information glut, along with the deification process,
has had a curiously ambiguous effect: it has informed us so
thoroughly about the life and character of the man that we
feel compelled to reexamine the work for evidence of the
virtues that would perhaps justify the attention and honor accorded the writer. Yet it has also made it impossible for us to
recapture that virginity of mind with which we first read him

From John W. Aldridge, "*The Sun Also Rises*—Sixty Years Later." First published in the
*Sewanee Review*, vol. 94, no. 2, Spring 1986. Copyright 1986 by John W. Aldridge.
Reprinted with permission of the editor and the author.

and were able to appreciate, without the inflammations of awe and reverence, the many excellent features of his artistry. For now we are confronting not a writer but an international literary monument, and the works that once seemed real and alive have become—as Mary McCarthy so admirably said about Salinger's Glass family writings—"the sacred droppings of holy birds." There is much irony in the fact that Gertrude Stein foresaw it all while meaning something else altogether when she observed that Hemingway "looks like a modern and he smells of the museums." And it is in the museum showcases of the world's adoration, among the Egyptian mummies, the ancient relics and artifacts, that Hemingway's works are now forever on public view. To extricate them from the museums and restore them to life is an impossible task. But with a sufficiently vigorous exercise of imagination it may be possible to approach them once again and ask some of the first questions, the kind that, in our virginity of mind, we were once able to answer, and that all the subsequent celebrity has almost caused us to forget how to ask.

## HEMINGWAY'S MOST SEDUCTIVE ATTRIBUTE

What was it then, and what is it now, that makes Hemingway so compellingly attractive as a writer; what is the nature and source of the very great pleasure we take in him when he is at his best, and the pain we feel when he is at his worst? To begin with the obvious and accepting the pretense that we are reading him for the first time, let us say that Hemingway's initially most seductive attribute was and remains his powerful responsiveness to experience. It is an attribute perhaps made more seductive by the fact that most of us since his time have found it to be seriously diminished in ourselves. One reason is that our responses to the infinitely more complex and diffuse experiences of our present world have *had* to diminish if we are to retain our sanity. Another reason is that so few of us today have, or have ever had, access to a clearly defined microcosmic world in which the things one feels, says, and does might take on the sacramental importance they had for Hemingway in the first [world] war, in Paris, and later in Spain. It is as if we had all suffered some brain damage as the price we have had to pay for existence in the second half of the century, a loss of acute responsiveness to the life around us, even as our sense that the vitality of that life has itself declined forces us into a troubled and abstracted self-preoccupation.

One does not easily envy the life of any of our immediate contemporaries—the talent, perhaps, but not the life—as one so easily envies Hemingway's, particularly during the years when his talent was freshest and he was writing at the top of his form in those early stories and *The Sun Also Rises*, his first and, withal, still his best novel. He was young then, as we were young when we first read him. He was living, as we regrettably were not, in the most exotic city in Europe among some of the most remarkable personalities and gifted artists of the post–World War I era. And he brought to it all the highly sensitized perspective of the provincial Midwestern tourist viewing with wonder and delight the hitherto undiscovered riches of foreignness.

He took the greatest pleasure—and gave us, vicariously, the greatest pleasure—in the hotels, bars, and restaurants of Paris, and with his quickly acquired inside-dopester knowingness, he appointed himself the official instructor in where and how to live wisely and well. He could recite the names of all the streets; he knew the exact location of all the good places and the best route to take to get to them; and he was on friendly terms with the best bartenders and waiters who worked in them. He had a wonderful eye not only for quality but for terrain, whether the topography of Paris or the landscape of Spain, and in sharing his knowledge with us, he schooled us in the ways of a world we did not know but desperately wished we did.

## THE LITERAL MANUFACTURE OF A WORLD

He also accomplished something far more significant for us and for literature. If he had not, then Scott Fitzgerald's well-known description of *The Sun Also Rises* as "a romance and a guidebook" might have been all that needed to be said. But in introducing us literally to the life of foreignness, Hemingway at the same time created the illusion that *every* element of life is in fact foreign, hence new and without precedent in the known experience of the past. Every element needs, therefore, to be carefully examined and tested to determine the degree of its authenticity. In order to live an authentic life and produce an authentic fiction, one has to proceed with the greatest caution and select only those experiences, express only those emotions, that have proved their validity because they have been measured against the realities of honest feeling and what one senses in one's deepest instincts to be true. The result in Hemingway's fiction is not a realistic reflection of a world but the literal manufacture of a world, piece by piece, out of the most meticulously chosen and crafted materials.

It is a world that is altogether strange and perilous because it is without moral history and received standards of conduct. Characters, therefore, must move through it as if through enemy-held territory, learning how to live while trying to stay alive. To survive they need all the cunning and expertise they can muster. They must be sure that they know at all times exactly where they are, both geographically and in relation to others. They must also learn exactly how to behave so as to minimize the risk of becoming vulnerable to error and the dangerous consequences of losing self-control. They must fabricate, through constant study and trial, an etiquette that will enable them to know instinctively what is appropriate and what is not, so that they can maintain decorum under stress or siege. They must master the procedure for everything, the correct methods for carrying out their function—whether it is hunting, fishing, bullfighting, or eating and drinking. And above all they must know the cost of everything, not only the cost in money but the physical and emotional cost. To survive successfully is to learn how to get one's money's worth, the right return on the investment; hence, one must be extremely careful to make only the *right* investments, those that will yield honest satisfactions and beneficial emotions rather than lead to the overinflation of specious values and destructive emotions. . . .

## THE PRECISE LANGUAGE OF A MORALLY FASTIDIOUS WORLD

Hemingway's tight minimalist style, which is displayed in its purest form in *The Sun Also Rises*, is the precise verbal expression of the view of life that dominates and finally evaluates the action of the novel. If Hemingway believed, as he clearly did, that if the right, carefully selected experiences are chosen and only the proper emotions expressed, the result will be an absolutely authentic fictional world containing nothing that will ever ring false, then the language, chosen with equal care, so authentically simple and basic, is the perfect fastidious statement of the morally fastidious world it is designed to create. The vacant spaces between and behind the words, the strongly sensed presence of things omitted, become expressive of all the alternatives and elaborations, all the excesses and equivocations of language, that have been scrupulously rejected in the style's formation. The emphasis given to the individual words and phrases that seem so much larger than they are just because they have escaped rejection makes it appear that a verbal artifact is being constructed or salvaged, word by word, from a junk-heap of redundancy and imprecision. There are no moral or literary precedents to provide the style with foundation or scaffolding. Everything that manages, against great resistance, to achieve utterance is seemingly being uttered for the very first time in human history, is a kind of Ur-statement of primordial truth. It is a method whose ultimate effect is incantatory and catechistic, and what is being prayed to and propitiated is the demon god of flux and excess, that force of anarchy that drives most of the characters toward ruin and that it is the task of the language to redeem and convert into a force of artistic order.

Such a method, composed as it is of a minimum of simple words that seem to have been squeezed onto the page against a great compulsion to be silent, creates the impression that those words—if only because there are so few of them—are sacramental, while the frequent reappearance of some of them in the same or in similar order at intervals through the text tends to give them idiographic value. Thus, "nice" and the phrase "one of us" become the pervasive but hollow designations of moral judgment in the novel, and the hollowness is perfectly consonant with the theme. In a similar way, some of the characters become idiographs when a certain distinctive feature of their appearance or behavior is established in our minds as their identifying logo or psychological autograph—again because Hemingway describes them so sparingly that what little he does say about them takes on something of the quality of Homeric epithet. Thus, Jake is personified by his impotence, Bill Gorton by his passion for stuffed animals, Brett by her mannish hats and hairstyle, the Count by his arrow wounds, Robert Cohn by his romanticism. In each case, furthermore, the defining detail becomes revelatory of the character's dramatic role and thematic meaning, so that what begins as a novel of manners ends as a moral allegory about people who lack the moral substance even to follow the code of behavior which they profess to honor. Jake is unmanned and Brett is defeminized. Bill Gorton's passion is for things that look like the real thing but are actually dead. The Count has been wounded by arrows, which must make him as anachronistic as his fancy title and tastes supported by income from a chain of sweet-shops must make him ludicrous.

Brett with her title is also an anachronism, as is Mike, the stereotypical wastrel aristocrat with his stereotypical prospects of one day inheriting a fortune. And Cohn's romanticism, which is the central irritant in the novel, is yet another. All represent former sources of value that no longer have value. Cohn's sentimentalized vision of love belongs to that part of the 19th Century that was supposedly killed in the first world war, and its resurrection in the aftermath can only mean trouble for people who are also resurrected casualties, stuffed human animals, to whom any feeling, when aggressively acted upon, is a threat to psychic harmony and the security of non-feeling.

## AVOIDING EMOTION AND SENSORY STIMULI

In his study of American modernism, *A Homemade World*, Hugh Kenner makes the extremely perceptive observation that "Hemingway's achievement ... consisted in setting down, so sparely that we can see past them, the words for the action that concealed the real action." There is abundant evidence for this everywhere in *The Sun Also Rises*. Jake's strength as a character derives in large part from his capacity for withholding information. We are constantly aware in the novel of the presence of what we are not told, of what Jake refuses to acknowledge and judge because it is too dangerous to make a judgment and thus bring the danger to the surface of consciousness. As Carl Jung wrote in *Psychology and Religion*:

> Consciousness must have been a very precarious thing in its beginnings.... Even an ordinary emotion can cause a considerable loss of consciousness. Primitives therefore cherish elaborate forms of politeness, speaking with a hushed voice, laying down their weapons, crouching.... Before people of great authority we bow with uncovered head, i.e., we offer our head unprotected in order to propitiate the powerful one, who might easily fall suddenly a prey to a fit of uncontrollable violence.

And Otto Fenichel says in *Psychoanalytical Theory of Neurosis* that "trauma creates fear of every kind of tension ... because even a little influx of excitement may have the effect of 'flooding' the patient," or, in Jung's terms, causing him to lose consciousness and go berserk.

For the elaborately polite because clearly traumatized characters of this novel, consciousness is so precarious and fragile that any kind of tension is to be feared and, if possible, ignored. One can safely respond to only the barest minimum of sensory stimuli—the look of the landscape, the physical pattern of an action especially when strictly ritualized, what people monosyllabically said to one another. But there must be little or nothing revealed about how anyone really felt, what deeper emotions were aroused by the various conflicts and confrontations. It is part of the magic of the minimalist style that we know almost nothing—and we scarcely miss knowing—about Jake's emotional state throughout the major part of the novel, nor do we know much of anything about the nature of the relationship between Brett and Mike and between Jake and Bill. This information is carefully withheld or we are led to believe that it is revealed in actions that occur in the background or off-stage. But the omissions make a statement that there is some acute unpleasantness here that cannot be directly confronted because it is a threat to psychic equilibrium and might cause a dangerous "flooding" of consciousness. . . .

### HIS REAL LESSON IN HEROISM

Gertrude Stein, in one of her famous pronouncements on Hemingway, said that there is in fact a real story to be told about Hemingway, one that he should write himself, "not those he writes but the confessions of the real Hemingway." Clearly, Hemingway did not write it and could not because the real story was too deeply disturbing to tell, just as the young Nick Adams could not bring himself to enter the shadowy part of the river where it ran into the swamp—because "in the swamp fishing was a tragic adventure." But the remarkable fact is that in telling as much or as little of the story as he did, Hemingway managed through his complex artistry to use words in such a way that we are indeed allowed to see past them and to glimpse the outlines of the mysterious and probably tragic adventure that the words were not quite able to describe but were also not quite able to conceal.

If the thing most feared is barely visible behind the language, the fear itself is barely controlled by the language.

Language is a provisional barricade erected against the nihilism that threatens to engulf his characters, the nihilism that is always seeking to enter and flood the human consciousness. Hemingway at his best offered us a portrait that did not need to be painted of a condition we recognize everywhere around and within us, and he gave us as well our only means of defense against it—the order of artistic and moral form embodied in a language that will not, in spite of everything, give up its hold on the basic sanities, will not give up and let out the shriek of panic, the cry of anguish, that the situation logically calls for. That, and not any of the bravura exploits behind his celebrity, constituted his heroism, and that was the lesson in heroism he had to teach. Of his many qualities that was the one that most deserved, and continues to deserve, our admiration and loyalty.

# Anti-Semitism in *The Sun Also Rises*

Gay Wilentz

Robert Cohn is not merely an offensive cad; Hemingway deliberately makes him an offensive Jewish cad,
charges Gay Wilentz, essayist and women's studies
specialist. She points out that Hemingway, who does
not use superfluous words, frequently inserts "Jewish" in the epithets by which he and his other characters refer to Cohn. Hemingway seems to hold Cohn—
outsider, alien, immigrant—responsible for devaluing
the world in which "manly" virtues created success.
Instead, the unmasculine Cohn succeeds by preying
on the weakness of society in a postwar world that
Hemingway ultimately (by his suicide) rejected.

Carlos Baker, in his exhaustive study, refers to a statement
Hemingway made during a dinner party at which Harold
Loeb, one of the hangers-on of the Lost Generation set, was
a guest. Hemingway told the group about the new novel he
was writing: "I'm putting everyone in it and that kike Loeb is
the villain." Of course the book he was referring to is *The
Sun Also Rises*, and Harold Loeb was the inspiration for the
character Robert Cohn. Critical examinations of this classic
American novel have also been exhaustive, yet discussions
of Cohn have been peripheral at best and have not dealt
clearly with the thematic use of anti-Semitism in the novel.
Critics appear to fall into four main schools of thought on the
relationship of Cohn's Jewishness to his role as "offensive
cad," as Alan Tate calls him: 1) those, such as the two Bak-
ers, Carlos and Sheridan, who emphasize the biographical
details of the time and see the portrayal as a way to get back
at Loeb; 2) those, a few Jewish critics like Michael Hoffman
and Robert Meyerson, who focus solely on the anti-Semitic
portrait and on Hemingway's own dislike of Jews; 3) those

From Gay Wilentz, "(Re)Teaching Hemingway: Anti-Semitism as a Thematic Device in
*The Sun Also Rises*," *College English*, February 1990. Copyright 1990 by the National
Council of Teachers of English. Reprinted with permission.

who try to attribute some other reasons for Cohn being "not one of us" (Mark Spilka for example attributes the group's dislike of Cohn to his "Victorian notions," Larry Grimes calls him a failed "Don Quixote," and S.A. Cowan—turning even Jewish heritage against Cohn—calls him the "fool of Ecclesiastes"); 4) those, like Arthur Scott and Wolfgang Rudat, who totally misread the novel and call Cohn some sort of lost hero of the Lost Generation. My own purpose is not to discuss a well-worn and possibly useless question as to whether Hemingway was an anti-Semite nor to justify or condemn his portrayal of Cohn in the novel; rather I examine why Hemingway chose to make Jew-baiting an issue. . . . I contend that the meaningless world that Hemingway bemoans in *The Sun Also Rises* is filled with immigrants— identified in the Jew. Thematically, it is possible that this portrait of the Jewish male illustrates more than the Lost Generation and pre–World War II European society's attitudes towards Jews. Cohn may thus be seen as a symbol of the apprehensions that mainstream Americans had about an alien immigrant population in the early 20th century.

In *The Origins of Totalitarianism,* Hannah Arendt explains that the choice of Jews as the primary scapegoat of Nazi oppression was deliberate rather than arbitrary; as Meyerson points out, this is true of Hemingway's portrait of Cohn as well. Cohn is a fairly unlikeable character, possibly a despicable one (if you go by what the other characters say about him); the problem arises because Cohn is not just an "offensive cad" and a Jew—he is offensive because he is a Jew (although examples abound, a few choice ones should suffice): "He had a hard, Jewish, stubborn streak"; "Let him not get so superior and Jewish"; "Take that sad Jewish face away"; "What do you think it has meant to have that damned Jew about?"

Hemingway, known as a stylist who does not include superfluous words, would not have added "Jewish" as a descriptive adjective so many times without a purpose. My aim is to look at this purpose as part of Hemingway's thematic device. Robert Cohn works well as a foil to the protagonist Jake Barnes. Barnes, who is a "real man" by Hemingway's standards (he has grace under pressure, is an *aficionado,* and is both hard-boiled and vulnerable), is impotent because of a war wound—another symbol of "manliness"; ironically, it is the outwardly emasculated Cohn who can

perform, and if only for a short time, get the girl (Brett Ashley) that Jake can never have. Several other critics have seen
Cohn as a foil to Barnes. And certainly, there is validity in
exposing Cohn as holding chivalric notions that no longer
work in the modern world: Cohn's self-deception is coun-
tered by Jake's ability to face his own wounds. But this reading still does not address the question of why Hemingway
chose to portray Cohn as a Jew. In fact, the chivalric code is
based on Christian ideals and out of the range of traditional
Jewish culture anyway. Even in embracing the chivalric
code of the medieval knights, Cohn is trying to identify with
his gentile peers.

---

### AN IDEALIZED YOUNG "HEMINGSTEIN"

Robert Cohn, a case of "arrested development," partly because he missed the war, can easily move in to shatter
[Jake's posture of passive stoicism] by unwittingly violating
the code, forcing the group to recognize its lost options of
physical prowess and romantic love. Cohn, we might guess,
is an idealized version of the mediocre success young
"Hemingstein" might have become minus his baptism, and
for this he is treated with the contemptuous pity one feels
for old buoyant enthusiasms once they have been exploded
by the shock of reality.

Peter Stine, "Hemingway and the Great War," *Fitzgerald/Hemingway Annual*,
1979.

---

The opening few pages of the novel condemn Cohn to a
stereotypical portrayal. We find out that Cohn has won a
boxing title at Princeton, but quickly our narrator Jake dis-
pels any thoughts we'd have that he was committed to the
sport: "[The title] meant a lot to Cohn. He cared nothing for
boxing, in fact he disliked it, but he learned it painfully and
thoroughly to counteract the feeling of inferiority and shy-
ness he had felt on being treated as a Jew in Princeton." We
learn further that his obviously large Jewish nose was "per-
manently flattened" in a fight and that it "certainly improved
his looks." Cohn is from a *nouveau riche* New York family,
and that, of course, explains both his job as editor and the
publication of his book. He's none too bright, either, usually
taking his ideas from others, and then, to add insult to injury, he asks too many questions and is too intellectual in his

responses. He's sad and suffering, qualities alluded to as endemic to the race, and he isn't even politic enough to realize that he is the perennial outsider in this expatriate in-group. People like the drunk Harvey Stone call Cohn a "moron" to his face, and the characters (as well as the readers) blame Cohn. Cohn gets more than he deserves and stays when he isn't wanted; he is the emasculated Jewish male who succeeds in a world where the real men know it's not worth trying. He is a symbol of this post-war environment in that his success comes from preying on the weakness of a society devalued by the breakdown of pre-war values and ideals as well as industrialization. Alan Tate in a 1926 review of *The Sun Also Rises* states that Hemingway reduces certain characters (like Cohn and Brett) to caricatures and states further: "Robert Cohn is not only a bounder, he is a Jewish bounder. The other bounders, like Mike, Mr. Hemingway for some reason spares." The reason Cohn is not spared has much to do with his Jewishness, as Tate implies without elaboration. The other bounders—like Mike, Bill, and even Jake—are men and live by the "code"; even Brett acts more "manly" than Cohn at the bullfights. Cohn's lack of manliness, inability to comprehend the larger issues, maladroitness, and hen-pecked personality reflect Hemingway's fears of the disorderliness of a post-war, industrialized society—a society where those without the basic tenets of American manhood can be usurpers. And the ultimate example of this usurpation is that Cohn takes Brett to bed whereas Jake can't. . . .

Cohn's relationship with Jake is pitiful. Cohn, obviously friendless for the most part, is overjoyed to be befriended by Jake, whom everyone admires. More than once he calls Jake—who insults him, sits by when others insult him, and talks about him behind his back—his best friend. The fact that both of them love Brett adds to Jake's disdain for Cohn. At first, Jake finds Cohn's uncomfortableness and effeminate adoration of Brett rather amusing. When he sees Cohn first looking at Brett, Jake tells us: "He looked a great deal as his compatriot must have looked when he saw the promised land." To Cohn, Brett represents the "shiksa" all Jewish men aspire to—not merely "trés, trés gentille" as Jake's concierge notes but also gentile. When Cohn crosses that well-known line, however, Jake begins to hate him—not Mike, not the others who have slept with Brett, not Romero, but Cohn. It is Cohn who tries to push in where he is not wanted, who has committed a sin so bad that even the woman whom he "de-files" states after sex with Romero, "I'm all right again. He's wiped out that damned Cohn." After the aborted fight, when he attacks Jake for pimping between Brett and Romero, Cohn cries and begs Jake to forgive him. Cohn tells Jake, "You were the only friend I had," but all Jake notices is that he's wearing the same kind of (immature) polo shirt he wore at Princeton. We might feel sorry for Cohn if we weren't al-ready sick of his whining. By having sex with Brett and see-ing it as a sign of a romantic attachment, Cohn has thrown Jake's disability in his face.

## PHYSICAL VS. EMOTIONAL EMASCULATION

Jake's wound, which in some ways represents not only the horrors of the great war but also the notions surrounding what makes a man, is a unifying image for the novel. Jake is a man in spite of or because of his impotence. He was being a "man"—fighting for his country—when it happened. Cohn, on the other hand, is physically sound but emotion-ally emasculated. He doesn't go to war, he's picked on by both wife and girlfriend, he turns green at the bullfights, and of course, he turns down the fishing trip to be with Brett, de-spite the fact she does not want him either. This image of the American Jewish male as both usurping and effeminate is further emphasized by Brett's boyfriend Mike's attack on Cohn: "I would have thought you'd love being a steer, Robert. . . . They never say anything and they're always hanging around so." In no way does Cohn act like a man. Later, Mike reinforces this connection as he tells the others: "Brett's gone off with men before. But they weren't ever Jews and they didn't come and hang about afterward." Even Jake, who is clearly used to seeing Brett with other men, is horri-fied at the thought of her having an affair with Cohn.

But of course we know that it isn't Robert Cohn who is the "steer"; it's Jake, so to speak. This is the supreme irony. Jake, who typifies all the traditional values of manhood, is unable to fulfill his greatest desire. There are suppositions by critics as to why Hemingway made Jake impotent, but it is evident that having the Jew Cohn go off with Brett is the last blow to his weakened manhood. The Jewish usurper, who has so often functioned as antithetical to true Christian values since before the Middle Ages, is once again disrupting a world already shaken. As Meyerson comments, Cohn is a "devalue-er" of tradition. And the traditions that Hemingway appears to hold Cohn responsible for devaluing are not necessarily the human values that the war has destroyed, but rather the American naturalist traditions of a pre-industrial world. Cohn, as representative of a devalued, outsider, immigrant society, refuses to accept a second-class position. He does not stay in his place and in that sense he challenges a social caste system weakened seriously by industrial development in the US and the war in Europe. Arendt notes that the Jews, "caught up in the general and insoluble conflicts of the time, could be blamed for them and finally be made to appear the hidden authors of all evils." She goes on to say that after World War I certain anti-Semites put forth a rumor that the Jews caused the war. Whether Hemingway was aware of this is unknown, but that was the climate which surrounded these post-war expatriates. Moreover, this sentiment can be easily applied to conflicts facing a newly industrialized America as well. Finally, since much of the focus of the novel is on how the "Great War" has crippled people physically and psychologically, it is not hard to see that Cohn, a Jew who did not fight for his country, might represent all that is wrong in this post-war society. . . .

## AN UNWANTED, CHAOTIC FUTURE

Beyond reflecting the prevailing attitudes towards Jews in pre–World War II Europe, Hemingway's treatment of Robert Cohn symbolizes a chaotic future of which Hemingway wanted no part. Like other Anglo-Americans at the time, he probably felt threatened by the hordes of immigrants entering his country through Ellis Island. This fear and disgust towards these aliens was coupled with an equal distrust of a society based on industry—a society where physical strength and raw masculinity would be less valuable than business know-how. Add to that the suspect role of the Jew in Christian society, and it is conceivable that he saw Cohn as a harbinger of things to come. Although Hemingway does not articulate the values of a pre-industrial time, it is clear what he doesn't want—an alien population who could succeed without any of the breeding, manliness, and finesse of Anglo-Americans. Jake's impotence symbolizes his consciousness of the meaninglessness of the modern day world; here is a world in which what has made man a potent being, a conqueror of nature, no longer matters. In this world, the Jews

# Women and Minorities in *To Have and Have Not*

Jeryl J. Prescott

Hemingway liked strong but not domineering women, and many of his works exhibit a sympathy for the plight of women, notes English professor Jeryl J. Prescott. His depictions of Helen and Marie in *To Have and Have Not* contrast favorably with that of the insensitive Richard Gordon. However, Hemingway's treatment of women differs significantly from that of minorities—Cubans and Africans—in the novel, who are consistently devalued and used as foils to increase the stature of the white hero.

Vulnerable to the whims of its vessel, language discloses or conceals, clarifies or obscures, supports or subverts. Hemingway's talents allow him to operate across these scales as he searches for venues to illustrate and test his code. In *To Have and Have Not*, however, it is the venue, not the code, that occupies the author's attention. Though definite references to the code are intrinsic to the novel, the more pressing task for Hemingway involves lifting the proverbial veil of the democratic myth—the sexual equality rhetoric and the human interest pretense—and allowing the participants in this facade to see the true picture. Ultimately, his depictions illuminate the persistent consciousness of the demarcations between "us" and "them" which foster division and prejudice in our society. . . .

Hemingway presents the protagonist's story and the stories of other Cuban/Floridian inhabitants without the curtains of meaningless discourse of sexual and racial equality. Instead, he uses unlocked, unexplained, unapologetic language. While showcasing this culture and its language, Hemingway continues his policy of omission by never directly addressing ethnic and gender social issues; thus he strengthens

From Jeryl J. Prescott, "Liberty for Just(us): Gender and Race in Hemingway's *To Have and Have Not*," *CLA Journal*, December 1993. Reprinted by permission of The College Language Association.

the story by making readers experience more than they consciously understand. He even goes further; he makes use of feminist rhetoric of rage, economy of stereotype, and metonymic displacement [using the name of one object or concept for another to which it is related] to illuminate perceived gender and ethnic differences within a society that professes to foster equality yet frowns on difference. Ironically, Hemingway uses literary techniques which depend on the sexist and racist conditioning of his reading audience.

In "Hemingway's Women's Movement," an article by Charles Nolan, the author notes numerous examples from Hemingway's works that indicate his recognition of gender inequities. "Whatever his personal idiosyncrasies (and there were many), as a writer he saw more clearly than perhaps even he knew." Nolan examines Hemingway's short stories and a couple of his novels. The critic begins with "Cat in the Rain," a deceptively simple story about a young, American, married couple vacationing in Italy. As her husband reads, the wife looks out of a window and notices a cat crouching underneath a table to evade the rain. Motivated by compassion as well as boredom, she decides to go get the cat, but the cat was no longer there. She therefore returns to the room. Still reading, the husband shows little concern for her or the cat. Eventually, he tells her to "shut up and get something to read."

The husband's crass words in conjunction with his unattentive attitude characterize him as a stereotypical male who sees little benefit in taking his wife seriously. Her needs seem uncomplicated, even meager, yet he ignores them. Hemingway juxtaposes the husband's cold, distant, inactive nature with that of the padrone, whom the wife "liked" because of his "dignity," "the way he wanted to serve her," and the "deadly serious way he received any complaints." As the story concludes, the padrone sends the cat to the wife's room, a simple and effortless gesture, to supply a surrogate for "fun" and "long hair," examples of the wife's modest desires.

Jig, the woman in "Hills Like White Elephants" finds herself with a similarly unresponsive male. Apparently, she is pregnant and they are discussing their options. The man, whose namelessness implies a universality, encourages her to have an abortion, "an awfully simple operation." Nolan explains that the man "wants their essentially shallow relationship to continue as it has." On the other hand, Jig seems tired of the many nights in hotels and the one-dimensional

relationship. The man's selfishness and inconsiderate behavior illuminates Jig's unappreciated position as a member
of this relationship and, furthermore, of society.

Nolan's observations lead him to the following conclusion: "Throughout [Hemingway's] work up to the late thirties, there runs a strong sympathy for the plight of women, a
sympathy that at one point, in fact, is expressed in feminist
rhetoric and rage." This expression occurs in *To Have and
Have Not.*

## STRONG WOMEN

Linda Miller notes (in "Hemingway's Women: A Reassess-
ment") that "Hemingway did not like domineering women,
yet he admired strong women." In *To Have and Have Not,*
Helen represents one of Hemingway's stronger women. At
the end of an obviously unhealthy relationship, Helen and
Richard Gordon play out the bitter end to their marriage.
Helen reveals that they did not marry in a church, that she
has had an abortion, that their sex life is full of "dirty little
tricks," and that her "heart . . . [is] broken and gone." She
concludes that "love is just another dirty lie." Helen's summary of her marriage parallels Hemingway's postmodernist
summary of the world. Unsanctioned by the church, their
marriage lacks a moral history. Her abortion and subsequent indications of a hysterectomy indicate the sterility of
the world. Helen emerges from this marriage hopeless and
faithless. With complete cynicism, she lumps "love" in with
every other destroyed belief; it is "just another dirty lie."
Helen directs her statements at one man, but [as Nolan
notes] "it is hard to read the passage without hearing in the
background the condemnation of all men" as well as the resignation to a morally glutted world.

Also a product of this world, Richard Gordon sees women
stereotypically. Richard, a writer, briefly observes Marie
Morgan and decides to model a character after her. Nevertheless, his perceptions about Marie are all wrong:

> Her husband when he came home at night hated her, hated
> the way she had coarsened and grown heavy, was repelled by
> her bleached hair, her too big breasts, her lack of sympathy
> with his work as an organizer. He would compare her to the
> young, firm-breasted, full-lipped little Jewess that had spo-
> ken at the meeting that evening. It was good. It was, it could
> be easily, terrific, and it was true. . . . Her early indifference to
> her husband's caresses. Her desire for children and security.

> Her lack of sympathy with her husband's aims. Her attempts
> to simulate an interest in the sexual act that had become ac-
> tually repugnant to her. It would be a fine chapter.

Actually, Harry Morgan's admiration of his wife's appearance
and his sexual satisfaction with her are obvious. When she
expresses insecurity about her age, her looks, and her sexuality—there is also an intimation that Marie has had a hysterectomy—Harry reassures her that she will "never be old."
With brutish affection, he tells her, "You're some old woman."
While there is no indication that she does not love their two
daughters, she clearly sympathizes with Harry's sexual, emotional, and professional needs. Obviously, Richard's misread-
ing of Marie in conjunction with his failed marriage implies
that his perceptions of women as frigid, insecure, objectified
"others" prohibits his ability to relate to them. His alienation
from women prefaces his eventual alienation from the world.
Through Richard, Hemingway exhibits uncensored male
perceptions of females perhaps as a partial explanation for
why women occupy subjugated positions in American society. His depictions affirm, and then refute, society's messages
about gender roles and characteristics.

## TREATMENT OF MINORITIES

Curiously, Hemingway's treatment of women in *To Have
and Have Not* differs significantly from his treatment of minorities. Also relegated to the fringes of society, ethnic minorities function as convenient pawns for Hemingway and
his characters to manipulate. Toni Morrison in *Playing in
the Dark: Whiteness and the Literary Imagination* asserts
that the essential themes of American literature—"auton-
omy, authority, newness, and difference"—depend on an
Africanist presence for their existence, and this presence
haunts *To Have and Have Not.*

In this critical work by the noted fiction writer, Morrison
posits that "race has become metaphorical—a way of referring to and disguising forces, events, classes, and expressions of social decay and economic division far more threatening to the body politic than biological 'race' ever was."
Similar to the practice of minstrelsy, in which "a layer of
blackness applied to a white face releases it from law,"
American writers engage in a parallel practice by employing
"an imagined Africanist persona to articulate and imaginatively act out the forbidden in American culture." Morrison

remains convinced that "the metaphorical and metaphysical uses of race occupy definitive places in American literature, in the 'national' character, and ought to be a major concern of the literary scholarship" surrounding this literature. . . .

---

### No Need for Real African-Americans

My interest in Ernest Hemingway becomes heightened when I consider how much apart his work is from African-Americans. That is, he has no need, desire, or awareness of them either as readers of his work or as people existing anywhere other than in his imaginative (and imaginatively lived) world. I find, therefore, his use of African-Americans much more artless and unselfconscious than Poe's, for example, where social unease required the servile black bodies in his work.

Toni Morrison, *Playing in the Dark: Whiteness and the Literary Imagination,* 1992.

---

In *To Have and Have Not,* Hemingway uses minority presence, what Morrison refers to, specifically, as an Africanist presence, "as a fundamental fictional technique" by which he establishes Harry Morgan's character and reveals a national character of European superiority and minority subjugation. I would extend Morrison's thesis, in this case, to include Cubans, the other minority presence operating within this novel.

Early in the novel, Harry meets the three Cubans in a cafe in Havana to discuss taking them to the United States. He explains to the "fellows" that he is unwilling to risk carrying them across the border illegally. As they realize that Harry is not willing to risk taking them, they become "angry" while Harry remains calm—his calmness amplified by the constant elevation of the Cubans' anger. Harry characterizes their attitudes as "nasty." Without any evident justification, Harry says, "I'm sure you've cut plenty people's throats," further emphasizing and establishing the stereotype of Cuban brutality. One Cuban responds, "I would like to kill you," affirming his preestablished nature. Still, Harry remains calm, sincere, rational; he even apologizes.

As the Cubans leave the cafe and enter the street in front of the cafe, Harry hears gunshots and hides quickly. The narrator, Harry at this point in the novel, tells us that one gunman is "a nigger." The other, wearing "a chauffeur's white duster," is assumed to be white because the narrator does not say otherwise. Suddenly, as the "nigger" appears on the scene, the angry, throat-cutting, ready-to-kill-Harry Cubans become "boys," a word connoting innocence and vulnerability. The chauffeur never kills anyone; he simply shoots at them, missing, until he is killed. Meanwhile the "nigger" carries out the three brutal murders of the now-characterized-as-helpless Cuban "boys." Before Pancho, one Cuban boy is shot, he kills the chauffeur. Pancho's face is "white as a dirty sheet" before "the nigger" shoots him "in the belly" and blows "the side of his head off." With characteristic Hemingway understatement, Harry utters, "some nigger."

## THE CHARACTERIZATION OF HARRY

In this scene alone we see two of the strategies Morrison identifies. Economy of stereotype ("nigger," a sexless, nameless term, gets no further description) and metonymic displacement (the chauffeur in "white" kills no one and remains innocent, relative to his "black" partner) invoke all of the racial connotations inherent in American society. Moreover, these techniques complement Hemingway's writing traits by allowing omission, supporting imagism, and by increasing the impressionistic view of his characters' world. Concurrently, these scenes juxtapose the just-introduced Harry with other despicable characters, resulting in the formation of admiration for the protagonist, who goes "clean around the outside of the square" following the violence.

Harry is further characterized as competent and authoritative in the following scene in which Hemingway goes to extraordinary measures to keep the African crew member silent. While taking a customer fishing on the boat, Harry, Eddy (a drunk incompetent), Johnson (the customer), and Wesley (an African man) comprise the crew. While Eddy rests, Harry and Johnson fish from the side of the boat. Meanwhile, Wesley steers the boat, the only person facing the direction in which the boat moves. At a crucial moment, Hemingway needs a character to recognize "a patch of flying fish." While it would seem natural for Wesley to yell out, he does not. Instead, Harry says, "I looked and saw he had seen a patch of flying fish burst out ahead and up the stream a little."

Morrison points out that "enforcing the silence of the 'nigger' proves problematic," resulting in a construction that is "improbable in syntax, sense, and tense." The obvious questions are how does one see that someone has already seen and why couldn't Wesley simply cry out at the sighting? Because, as Morrison states, "it is the powerful one, the authoritative one, who sees."

Harry is further characterized by contrast with an Africanist presence when Harry and Wesley are returning on the boat, both wounded, from stealing cases of liquor. The African speaks a great deal in this chapter but strictly for the purpose of winning admiration for Harry. Throughout this scene, Harry displays concern for Wesley, compassion, strength, patience, kindness, and complete emotional equilibrium in his wounded state. Afterward, Harry loses his arm and never even comments about the missing limb throughout the entire novel. In contrast, Wesley behaves by grumbling, whimpering, acting scared, childish, and ugly in response to his wound. The African man lacks grace under the pressure of pain, and he talks incessantly, violating the code of silence admired as well as adopted by Jake in *The Sun Also Rises*. In true cliché form, Wesley wallows in self-pity. He moves further into the world of the "other" as the scene nears its conclusion with Wesley "howling" and "blubbering," nonhuman noises. Morrison calls this collapse of Wesley into an animal—which prevents human contact—metaphysical condensation, a technique that "allows the writer to transform social and historical differences into universal differences." Again, the effect is impressionistic, blurring the boundary between human and animal as well as further dividing the world into "us" and "them."

The novel ends with yet another example of Hemingway's employment of an Africanist presence as well as further indications of the position of women in society. Marie Morgan, mourning Harry's death, thinks fondly of him "like he was, snotty and strong and quick, and like some kind of expensive animal":

> I remember that time he took me over to Havana when he was making such good money and we were walking in the park and a nigger said something to me and Harry smacked him, and picked up his straw hat that fell off, and sailed it about a half a block and a taxi ran over it. I laughed so it made my belly ache.

This passage reinforces Harry's status as a powerful, sexual protector. Notice that Marie does not remember what the

African man said; it is safe to infer from Marie's description that the content of his discourse was irrelevant. The mere fact that he spoke to her was enough. By speaking, he stepped beyond his bounds. Morrison explains:

> The disrespect, with its sexual overtones, is punished at once by Harry's violence. He smacks the black man. Further, he picks up the fallen straw hat, violating the man's property, just as the black man had sullied Harry's property—his wife. When the taxi, inhuman, onrushing, impartial machine, runs over the hat, it is as if the universe were rushing to participate in and validate Harry's response. It is this underscoring that makes Marie laugh, aloud with her obvious comfort in and adulation of this "strong and quick" husband of hers.

Other than the obvious inferior status of the African to Harry, this scene illuminates the position of women in society as property.

This scene is followed immediately with Marie's recollection of a beauty parlor visit during which she has her hair lightened. This transfer from dark to blond parallels a transformation from black to white. As she explains, the process becomes difficult; nevertheless, she emerges from the parlor successful. Marie's delightful response is clearly sensual as she touches it, describes its softness, her excitement, and her "funny" feeling inside. Harry's responses—"Jesus, Marie, you're beautiful" and "Don't talk about it . . . let's go to the hotel"—validate Marie's new sexual value.

Marie and Harry's perceptions of themselves and each other depend on social education about ethnicity and gender. Living on the fringe of poverty, they can elevate themselves in a society that devalues a race simply by juxtaposing themselves with that race. In addition, Marie's value is directly proportional to her sexuality and, specifically, a man's recognition and approval of it. Perhaps with clear anticipation of his audiences' conditioning, Hemingway manipulates his readers' desires to feel beautiful, powerful, free, and favored by the universe. . . .

## A NOTE OF HOPE?

Within the world of selfishness represented in Hemingway's canon, the "lost, lamented for values" include faith, hope, and security as well as "fertility, creativity, love, peace, and human brotherhood for maintaining life," as E.A. Lambadaridou writes. Through the author's exposé of the barren society in *To Have and Have Not*, he implies that these values cannot coexist with sexism and racism, two forces that foster hate, superficial evaluation, separatism, and general unrest. Harry's last words, "A man alone ain't got no bloody fucking chance," imply that togetherness may be the first step toward healing. Searching within the abyss of nada for meaning, people must first reform and embrace each other before they can reform and embrace the world.

# Hemingway's Humor

Sheldon Norman Grebstein

Most critics—influenced, perhaps, by the grim subject matter of much of Hemingway's writing—have failed to note that he was a masterful humorist, observes English professor Sheldon Norman Grebstein. Hemingway used many types of humor, including parody, mimicry, satire, and black humor. A sense of humor is an important trait for his characters— a vital component of the code that allows them to exhibit grace under pressure. Comedy is also woven into the structural design of the novels, as a counterpoint to the tragic elements.

At the end of the first chapter of *For Whom the Bell Tolls*, as Robert Jordan accompanies Pablo and Anselmo into the mountains to carry out the mission that could kill him, he counteracts his gloomy forebodings with a joke to himself and then goes on to formulate a principle for right conduct: "All the best ones, when you thought it over, were gay. It was much better to be gay and it was a sign of something too. It was like having immortality while you were still alive." Unquestionably Jordan speaks for Hemingway here and states a belief the writer himself strove to practice. In fact, there is a plenitude of gaiety in Hemingway's work, expressed in a comic vein which reaches from one end of his career to the other: from the contributions in high school periodicals to the posthumously published *A Moveable Feast* and *Islands in the Stream.* Furthermore, not only is this humor a vital attribute in those of Hemingway's characters who, like Jordan, exhibit grace under pressure, it is an important aspect of his craft. Yet with a very few exceptions the critics have neglected it.

Hemingway's humor encompasses a rather wide range of types, subjects, and moods. He was a skilled parodist and mimic who exercised his gift early and late. He wrote con-

From Sheldon Norman Grebstein, *Hemingway's Craft* (Carbondale: Southern Illinois University Press, 1973). Copyright ©1973 by Southern Illinois University Press. Reprinted with permission.

siderable satire, about equally apportioned between the gentle Horatian and the savage Juvenalian. Although much of his humor is dark—indeed so black it inhibits laughter—a good deal of it is also spontaneously and boisterously funny, with its major result the release of high spirits. He could be heavily and crudely obscene or profane, and just as delicately and subtly witty. In a few instances in his fiction the comedy seems forced and excessive, but in the main it is tightly integrated into the overall method and structure of the work and contributes significantly to its total achievement.

Hemingway's primary technique of humor, a technique which in itself articulates the comic vision, is that of incongruous juxtaposition. By this method contrasting or grossly unlike elements of attitude, language, action, or identity are placed in close proximity or paired in various combinations, so that surprise and laughter inevitably result from the absurd relationships and distortions produced by the unexpected arrangement of mismatched constituents. For example, one of Hemingway's favorite comic situations might be called nationality farce, which is really a version of the archetypal confusion-of-identity plot, wherein an American is mistaken for a German by an Italian, and so on. Another is to play off different speech patterns, modes of utterance, or language norms, and then capitalize on the attendant cacophony or misapprehension. The language-humor may collaborate in the nationality farce or it may function independently, as in the case which juxtaposes highbrow speech against the vulgate, or uses magniloquent terms to describe a low-down action or object. Another method stresses a character's silly or erratic behavior in circumstances which call for restraint and poise. Yet another technique sets incompatible values or attitudes side by side, usually so as to expose banal, pompous, or insincere thinking and conduct through the contrast with the frank, spontaneous, and earthy.

Although there are special instances in Hemingway's work of an entire piece which is deliberately and wholly comic, notably *The Torrents of Spring*, more typically Hemingway's humor functions as one component (albeit an important one) in an artistic whole. As a factor in characterization it adds depth and roundness. In plot it provides relief and foreshadowing. Structurally, it is a way to modulate and gain symmetry. Ultimately, of course, we must understand that Hemingway's humor is more than a mere device, stratagem, or overlay; it is integral to the particular image of life his work creates and fundamental to his mode of response. . . .

## PARODYING REAL PEOPLE

I surmise, without being able to prove my hunch, that some of the characterizations in the early chapters of *The Sun Also Rises* contain considerable parody of the speech-patterns of the characters' real-life prototypes. The substantiating evidence as well as the full appreciation of such parody would belong only to those who knew the people and had heard them talk. However, in some scenes, as for example the rendition of the homosexual group's dialogue in chapter 3, the parody is self-explanatory and requires no key. The same is true to some degree of Frances's excoriation of Robert Cohn at the end of chapter 6, a double-edged parody both of her personal style of speech and of Cohn's literary pretensions. There are also moments of parody included in Bill's two comic-satiric orations in chapter 12. The first parodies the fashionable clichés of literary criticism ("irony and pity") and jingoistic newspaper editorials ("You're an expatriate. You've lost touch with the soil."). The second is a burlesque sermon in the evangelistic manner of William Jennings Bryan, then at his most prominent because of his role in the Scopes Trial. In giving these parodic speeches to Bill, Hemingway was following actuality, for the character was in part modeled on Donald Ogden Stewart, an accomplished humorist and parodist who had recently published *A Parody Outline of History.*

Between *The Sun Also Rises* and *A Moveable Feast* the main inspiration for Hemingway's parodic humor was not so much individuals as attitudes embodied in certain kinds of utterance. For example, to name the most striking case in the short stories, there is the bleakly unfunny parody of the Lord's Prayer in "A Clean, Well-Lighted Place." In *Death in the Afternoon* the sequence of dialogues with the Old Lady, avowedly brought in for modulation and comic relief, depend essentially on parody. Although the Old Lady is herself a rather lovable character, her stilted formality, moral earnestness, and puzzled response to vulgar and unpleasant subjects comprise an extended parody of those academic and/or genteel readers and critics who had complained about Hemingway's crudity. Hemingway accentuates the parody of propriety by adopting a level of speech even loftier

than the Old Lady's, occasionally swooping down to under-
cut it with a snatch of obscenity, or by juxtaposing the po-
liteness of their style of conversation with such impolite top-
ics as the prevalence of venereal disease among matadors or
the practice of stuffing disemboweled horses with sawdust.
"A Natural History of the Dead," an extended and overt attack upon genteel critics, first emerged as one of these conversations. In it Hemingway parodies the propriety and objectivity of the field naturalist or travelogue writer (and, by
association, the literary critic) by adopting the manner of
sober decorum to describe the smell and posture of corpses
on the battlefield and similar matters. In another of these
conversations Hemingway paid an indirect compliment to
William Faulkner, then of far smaller reputation than Hemingway, as a writer *par excellence* about whorehouses.

### HEMINGWAY, THE WISE GUY

At the beginning of his career, it was the "wise guy" in
Hemingway who made an impression: Hemingway seemed
to be an extremely clever young man, possessing the special
callous cleverness of the police reporter and the tough guy.
To be a wise guy is to present an impudent, aggressive,
knowing, and self-possessed face or "front" to the world. The
most obvious mark of the wise guy is his sense of humor
which expresses his scorn and his sense of independence; he
exercises it as one of the best ways of controlling a situation
and of demonstrating his superiority to all situations.

Delmore Schwartz, "The Fiction of Ernest Hemingway," *Perspectives USA*, 1955.

The most insidious of all Hemingway's parody appears in
*A Moveable Feast*, where among others Gertrude Stein, Ford
Madox Ford, and F. Scott Fitzgerald are parodied not in their
literary practices but as individuals. That is, in each instance
Hemingway gets at his victim by the *ad hominem* method,
ridiculing personality and attitude rather than manner and
style. Yet these comic portraits also qualify as parody because they purport to precisely reproduce the person's
words as part of a dramatic scene, with Hemingway himself
in the role of innocent interlocuter and objective reporter.
Gertrude Stein is devalued because she first defends homosexuality as a viable way of life, a defense set down in digni-
fied and sophisticated terms as though recorded verbatim,

and then is later shown crawling abjectly before her lover. (Curiously, under the guise of fastidiousness, Hemingway does not report the second conversation but only hints at its substance.) Ford's pretensions to the status of gentleman are demolished by the word-by-word rendition of his petty bullying of a waiter and by his insupportably snobbish declarations. Hemingway ridicules Fitzgerald in the long anecdote about Fitzgerald's self-pitying hypochondria, and in the briefer but more devastating episode wherein Fitzgerald seeks Hemingway's reassurance about the adequacy of his sexual equipment. Although Hemingway takes care in all these scenes to avoid blatant exaggeration of personal mannerisms of speech, lest satire become burlesque and character lampoon, they are parody nonetheless. Much of this is amusing, even hilarious, but it is contemptible, too, in light of our knowledge that these were Hemingway's friends and sponsors. As a result we find ourselves in the uncomfortable predicament of despising Hemingway in the very moment that we laugh with him. . . .

## SATIRE IN *THE SUN ALSO RISES*

It is obvious, then, that Hemingway liked parody and did it well. However, as we have implied, parody really belongs to a broader comic dimension in Hemingway's work: satire. Each of Hemingway's novels contains at least some satire and it also recurs in a number of short stories. His targets are those satirists have ever aimed at, affectation and hypocrisy; his tone ranges from mild ridicule to scathing denunciation; his motive is exposure rather than improvement. I say this, that his satiric bent was more often than not destructive, to embarrass or indict rather than reform, because he had no plan or program to rectify the faults he revealed other than a generalized ideal of manly conduct. But this is not to say that his satire is any the less effective thereby. Swift had no social program either.

The urge to uncover folly and humiliate the foolish is clearly visible in *The Sun Also Rises*, which is, as Jackson Benson has verified, an extensively satirical book. Although the main butt of the satire is Cohn, even the protagonists Jake and Brett are made to seem a little foolish at times. If Cohn and other sentimentalists and litterateurs of his ilk behave fatuously, Jake and Brett also commit egregious errors of judgment and conduct. Indeed, of the whole cast of the novel's characters only Montoya and Romero wholly escape Hemingway's satirical depiction because they alone adhere consistently to their principles and conduct themselves with dignity. There are also moments of wide, overt, and jocose satire such as that in chapter 19, in Jake's reflections upon the difference between French and Spanish waiters, and by implication, between French and Spanish values.

But despite such humorous interludes in the novel, and there are many, the ultimate effect of the book and its satire is not merely amusing. In this we reiterate a basic truth about both Hemingway's satire and his "humor" at large. Theoretically, we can define *The Sun Also Rises* as comedy in the strict literary sense of that term: it concentrates on folly and misconduct; its characters are somewhat buffeted about but remain alive and well at the novel's conclusion— at least as well as they began; it displays the discrepancy between what is and what ought to be, or between the visionary and the actual; it focuses upon man in his social aspects; it shatters the illusions imposed by artificial or impractical standards; and it finally affirms the life-urge and man's thrust to survive and continue. But two crucial factors intervene to inhibit laughter. First, there is the intangible element of tone, or the cumulative effect of the nuances of style, dialogue, and gesture—and the pervasive tone of *The Sun Also Rises* is decidedly not merry. Second, there is the theme, as reinforced and articulated by the action, of frustration and loss. Or it could be said very simply that a novel whose plot and character relationships depend upon a man's sexual mutilation and a woman's compulsive promiscuity is unlikely to produce a feeling of exhilaration in its readers. Yet neither hero nor heroine really qualifies as tragic. They do *function*, in their way. What we need to accurately name *The Sun Also Rises* is a word unavailable in our critical vocabulary. Properly speaking, the book is neither a tragedy nor a comedy but an Irony. . . .

## THE COMEDY IS PART OF THE STRUCTURAL FABRIC

Comedy is not only an ever-present element in Hemingway's novels but also woven into their structural designs. Surely this is true of the three best: *The Sun Also Rises*, *A Farewell to Arms*, *For Whom the Bell Tolls*. In them humorous scenes, dialogues, or interior monologues set off the tragic elements, contrasted—and yet interlocked—with them in a way I think is singularly typical of Hemingway and integral to the special tone of his work. They provide in the structure the traditionally valuable service of "comic relief" and more. Note, for example, that among the several patterns of alternation and counterpoint which organize *For Whom the Bell Tolls*, humor is central. Once we look for it, we find it everywhere. I will give only a brief and partial summary.

In chapter 1 the danger of the bridge is juxtaposed against Golz's jokes about names, and Pablo's treachery is played off against Jordan's punning about the Jockey Club. In chapter 2 humorous exchanges with the gypsy and Pilar intersperse with continual allusions to death. In chapter 3 Jordan's profound conversation with Anselmo about the morality of killing is immediately succeeded by Agustín's luridly funny obscene outburst. In chapter 4 the tension aroused by Pablo's opposition to the mission of the bridge dissipates during Pilar's hilarious monologue about bullfighters. Chapter 6 lightens the serious subject of politics by means of Maria's *malentendus* [misunderstandings]. In chapter 8 Fernando's stupidity and Pilar's joyful account of Valencia help overcome the threat of the Fascist aircraft and the disheartening news that the secret attack is a subject of common gossip. And so on throughout the novel, although with a necessary diminution in the amount and frequency of the comedy as the action accelerates to its tragic finale. Yet even near the end the accumulating disaster is modulated by the frenzied humor of Andrés's attempt to get through the Loyalist outposts, against the opposition of sentries who want to settle the whole question of his identity by shooting him or tossing a hand grenade. Like "The Gambler, the Nun, and the Radio" this episode (chapter 36) could stand as a model illustration of the term "dark humor," for it is at once a travesty and of the utmost seriousness.

We could apply the same kind of analysis to *The Sun Also Rises* and *A Farewell to Arms*, with similar results in our discovery of the frequency, range, and intensity of humorous passages and humorous modes: from the clever comedy of manners in Jake's conversation with a pretentious young American novelist affecting British accent and suavity, to the black irony of Frederic Henry unawarely ordering a second helping of food and beer in a café while Catherine lies dying in childbirth. But there is no need to continue. The evidence can be found in the work by anyone who searches for it.

I have noticed a tendency in recent writing about Hemingway, perhaps influenced by the sad physical and mental deterioration of his last years, the ugly manner of his death, and the revelation of the less admirable facets of his personality, to conclude with the depiction of him as a ruined and tragic figure both as a man and as an artist. I prefer to end with a different emphasis, one that I hope will be increasingly justified by the perspective of time. I think he was above all a magnificent craftsman, and among his prime virtues was the ability to laugh.

# A Few Notes of Literary History on *A Farewell to Arms*

Carlos Baker

Bad luck may have helped make a great novel: The
first draft of *A Farewell to Arms*, which would have
been Hemingway's first novel, was stolen in Paris,
records Hemingway scholar and biographer Carlos
Baker. By the time he began to write the story again,
several years later, the author had matured, and the
real-life traumas of love and war that had inspired
the book could be viewed from a more objective perspective. It still took several tries to get the ending
right, though—the second-to-last attempt shows how
different the book would be with the "wrong" ending.

The literary history of *A Farewell to Arms* is of more than
common interest. Except for an accident, it might have been
Hemingway's first novel rather than his second. As early as
1922, more than four years before the publication of *The Sun
Also Rises*, he had begun to write a story about a young
American ambulance driver on the Italian-Austrian front
during the First World War. It seems to have been highly romantic in manner and conception. It was also written in a
prose style considerably more elaborate and adjectival than
the one we customarily associate with the young Hemingway. But this early version of the novel, such as it was, has
been missing these forty years. The probabilities are that it
long ago dissolved in the waters of a Parisian sewer or went
up in flames to kindle someone's kitchen fire in the slums of
the capital. For the valise in which it was being carried to
Hemingway by his young wife [Hadley] was stolen by a petty
thief in the Gare de Lyon in Paris one winter afternoon late
in 1922. With it went the typescripts and longhand copies of
several other early stories of Hemingway's—virtually all that

From Carlos Baker, "Ernest Hemingway: *A Farewell to Arms*," in *The American Novel:
From James Fenimore Cooper to William Faulkner*, edited by Wallace Stegner. Copy-
right ©1965 by Basic Books, Inc. Reprinted by permission of BasicBooks, a division of
HarperCollins Publishers, Inc.

he had written up to that time. Dismayed and disheartened by his loss, Hemingway did not again try to tell the Italian story until 1928, nearly ten years after the events on which the narrative is based had actually taken place.

Hemingway's own account of his second major attempt to write the novel is also rather dramatic, both geographically and domestically. Few books have been set down in such a variety of places. It was begun in Paris, and continued in Key West, Florida; Piggott, Arkansas; Kansas City, Missouri; and Sheridan, Wyoming. He finished the first draft while living on a ranch near Big Horn, Wyoming. During this period, his second wife, Pauline, was delivered of a son by Caesarean section in Kansas City, and while he was revising his first draft, his father committed suicide by shooting himself in Oak Park, Illinois. Hemingway said:

> I remember all these things happening and all the places we lived in and the fine times and the bad times we had in that year. But much more vividly I remember living in the book and making up what happened in it every day. Making the country and the people and the things that happened, I was happier than I had ever been.

... The special pleasure that Hemingway took in his work arose no doubt from his recognition of how much better this fresh new version of the novel was turning out than the one he had lost to the petty Parisian thief a half-dozen years before. Now, with the experience of a first novel behind him, and with more than twenty-five published short stories to his credit, he was at last in a position to do justice to his romantic subject. For in the meantime he had grown up to his task.

He was also succeeding in following a piece of advice he had once offered to his friend and fellow novelist, F. Scott Fitzgerald. If something has hurt you badly, he argued, you must find a way to use it in your writing. You had better not moan and complain about past or present difficulties or personal misadventures. Instead you must use your misfortunes as materials for fiction. If you can write them out, get them stated, it is possible to rid yourself of the soreness in your soul. ...

## A PAIR OF TRAUMATIC EVENTS

The pain and sorrow which he was now using in his novel were based on a double actuality: a pair of traumatic events from 1918–19, neither of which he had been able to forget, even had he wished to do so. The earlier of the two was his severe wounding [at Piave Front, where the Italians faced the Austrians] during the night of July 8, 1918. . . . Several men were killed outright; one had his legs severed. Although his own extremities were terribly wounded, Hemingway managed to carry the dying soldier back to the main trench, though as he did so Austrian flares lit the scene and a heavy machine gun opened up at knee level on the staggering boy with his bloody burden. Before his heroic journey was done, he had taken two more slugs in the legs. This was the first of the two soul-shaking experiences which he could never forget, and which he had been trying for ten years to embody in prose fiction.

### BEATEN UP IN A GOOD CAUSE

It gives you an awfully satisfactory feeling to be wounded; it's getting beaten up in a good cause. There are no heroes in this war. We all offer our bodies and only a few are chosen. They are the lucky ones. I am proud and happy that mine was chosen, but it shouldn't give me any extra credit.

Ernest Hemingway, quoted in the *American Red Cross Central Division Bulletin*, December 7, 1918.

The second of his memorable experiences was a love affair with an American Red Cross nurse in Milan. Her name was Agnes von Kurowsky. Besides being an excellent and experienced nurse, she was young, pretty, kind, and gay. When the boy was brought at last to the comparative quiet and luxury of the base hospital, Miss von Kurowsky was one of those assigned to his case. It was Hemingway's first adult love affair and he hurled himself into it without caution. He seems to have been wholly unaware of the banality of the situation in which the young war hero falls in love with his nurse. Even if he had thought of it in these terms, he would not have cared in the least. For he had managed to convince himself that he was finally and irrevocably in love.

In spite of the fact that they were often separated for varying intervals during the summer and fall of his recuperation, Hemingway saw as much of his nurse as regulations (and competition from his fellow-Americans) would allow. When he sailed for New York in January 1919, his head was full of plans to get a newspaper job, save some money, bring his girl back to the United States, and be married. The traumatic aspect of this experience was that his plans were smashed. After some soul-searching of her own, Agnes decided that it would be a mistake to let a wartime romance try to attain the settled actuality of a peacetime marriage. She was older than he, she was an excellent and dedicated nurse, and she was not at all sure that she wanted to give up so important a profession in order to become another American housewife. Hemingway had not been home very long when he received the letter in which she set forth her conclusions.

It was a severe blow to his pride. He reacted explosively. All her protestations availed nothing. He turned against her with masculine rage and rankling sorrow, even as he had turned toward her while he lay recuperating in the hospital. But he was never able or willing to forget her. Though he subsequently married four times, he kept Agnes' letters all his life. Among the many he had loved and won, she was a perennial reminder of one woman he had loved and lost. She took on the not very enviable status of the goddess who is worshiped while remaining unattainable. As the first love of his young manhood, she remained enshrined in an alcove of his consciousness until the day he died. . . .

## AN ALTERNATIVE CONCLUSION

As we approach the end of this demonstration, there is just time to consider one more point about *A Farewell to Arms*. This is the famous conclusion where Catherine dies and her lover says a silent farewell before he walks back to the hotel alone in the falling rain. For years it has been rumored that Hemingway rewrote the closing pages of the novel some thirty-seven times. The figure is very likely exaggerated. But whatever it was, there can be no doubt that Hemingway spent considerable effort on the conclusion, and that the final version, familiar to readers since 1929, is almost infinitely superior to the penultimate version, which has only recently come to light.

In the accepted and familiar version, Hemingway's hero stays with Catherine until her death. Then he goes out to speak to the surgeon: "Is there anything I can do tonight?" The doctor replies that there is nothing to be done and offers Henry a ride back to his hotel. Henry says that he will stay for a while at the hospital. "It was the only thing to do," says the surgeon, apologetically, speaking of the fatal Caesarean section. "The operation proved—"

"I do not want to talk about it," says Henry. The doctor goes away down the corridor and Henry opens the door to the room where Catherine's body lies.

"You can't come in now," says one of the nurses in charge.

"Yes, I can."

"You can't come in yet."

"You get out," says Henry. "The other one, too."

But after he has got them out and closed the door and turned off the light, he discovers that it is no good. It is like saying goodbye to a statue. After a while he goes out and leaves the hospital, and walks back to the hotel in the rain.

This is where the novel ends. Much has been made of this justly famous and tight-lipped conclusion. To many readers it has seemed to be one of the high points of lonely bereavement in modern fiction, a peak of tragic lostness from a generation which suffered thousands of similar deprivations during and after World War I. It has also been seen as the epitome of stoic acceptance of the inevitable. There can be no doubt that this was precisely the effect Hemingway sought to achieve during all his rewritings of the conclusion.

The penultimate version is another matter entirely, and it is very revealing. In place of the laconic interchange between Henry and the attending surgeon, the visit to the room to say goodbye, and the lonely walk back to the hotel in the rain, we have three quite different paragraphs. Henry talks about the difficulty of making funeral arrangements in a foreign country, then of the postwar destinies of the priest and Rinaldi and one or two more, and finally of the return to the hotel, where he falls asleep to awake in the morning to his sense of loss. All the sharp poignancy of the final version is here blunted and destroyed. What is worse, the words themselves seem moist with self-pity.

Hemingway wrote, in the simulated character of Frederic Henry:

> There are a great many more details, starting with my first meeting with the undertaker, and all the business of burial in a foreign country, and going on with the rest of my life—which has gone on and seems likely to go on for a long time.
> . . . I could tell how Rinaldi was cured of the syphilis and lived to find that the technic learned in wartime surgery is not of much practical use in peace. I could tell how the priest in our mess lived to be a priest in Italy under Fascism. I could tell how Ettore became a Fascist and the part he took in that or-

ganization. I could tell how Piani got to be a taxi-driver in New York and what sort of a singer Simmons became. Many things have happened. Everything blunts and the world keeps on. It never stops. It only stops for you. Some of it stops while you are still alive. The rest goes on and you go on with it. . . . I could tell you what I have done since March, 1918, when I walked that night in the rain back to the hotel where Catherine and I had lived and went upstairs to our room and undressed and slept finally, because I was so tired—to wake in the morning with the sun shining in the window; then suddenly to realize what had happened. I could tell what has happened since then, but that is the end of the story.

The difficulty with this conclusion is that it drowns us with words and moisture. The rather garrulous self-pity, so visible here, when we juxtapose it with the far more objective stoicism of the final version, offers us a hint that may be worth developing. It suggests what I believe to be true, that the stoicism of the last version was only a mask, adopted and assumed for dramatic show, while under it Hemingway's still wounded feelings were bleeding and suppurating almost as intensively as they had been doing ten years before. Within the short space of seven months, he had been badly smashed up in both war and love. Now, much later, his double wound of body and soul rose to the surface of his memory, and manifested itself in the trial conclusion which we have just examined.

There is no time to expand further upon the matter here. Yet the idea of the stoic mask, assumed as a façade to conceal the psychic warfare which is going on beneath, may help us to explain and to understand much of the braggadoccio which struck his detractors as all too apparent in Hemingway's later life. It may also explain his espousal of the stoic code as a standard of behavior—a standard to which he required all his later heroes to conform. But these are hypotheses better suited to the biographer than to the literary critic. If the next-to-last conclusion of *A Farewell to Arms* betrays a kind of psychological quicksand just below the surface, the final version does not. . . . Whatever Hemingway's future reputation, *A Farewell to Arms* will surely stand for at least another forty years as the best novel written by an American about the First World War.

# CHRONOLOGY

## 1898
Marcelline Hemingway, Ernest's older sister, born January 15.

## 1899
Ernest Miller Hemingway born in Oak Park, Illinois, second of six children of Clarence Edmonds Hemingway, M.D., and Grace Hall Hemingway, July 21.

## 1902
Ursula Hemingway, Ernest's second sister, born April 29.

## 1904
Madelaine Hemingway, called Sunny, Ernest's third sister, born November 28.

## 1911
Carol Hemingway, called Beefy or Beefish, Ernest's fourth sister, born July 19.

## 1914–18
World War I; the United States enters the war in 1917.

## 1915
Leicester Clarence Hemingway, called Lester de Pester (later shortened to the Pest) by his only brother, Ernest, born April 1.

## 1917
Graduates from Oak Park High School. Possibly rejected by the army because of an eye injury (received while boxing?). (He may have only assumed he would be rejected, and his bad vision may have predated his attempts at boxing.) Works as a cub reporter for the *Kansas City Star* through April 1918. Eighteenth Amendment to the U.S. Constitution makes alcoholic beverages illegal.

## 1918
Goes to Italy as a Red Cross ambulance driver. July 8—Severely injured by mortar fragments near Fossalta di Piave, in Italy near the Austrian front. November 11—World War I ends.

## 1919

Treaty of Versailles.

## 1920

F. Scott Fitzgerald publishes *This Side of Paradise*. Women are given the right to vote by constitutional amendment. "Red scare" leads to arrest of twenty-seven hundred American Communists.

## 1920–24

Works as a reporter and foreign correspondent for the *Toronto Star* and *Toronto Star Weekly*.

## 1921

Marries Hadley Richardson; leaves for Europe.

## 1921–22

War between Greece and Turkey; Hemingway's first war correspondence in 1922.

## 1925

Fitzgerald publishes *The Great Gatsby*. Sherwood Anderson publishes *Dark Laughter*.

## 1926

Hemingway publishes *The Torrents of Spring* (a parody of Anderson's *Dark Laughter*) and *The Sun Also Rises*.

## 1927

Divorces Hadley Richardson and marries Pauline Pfeiffer.

## 1928–38

Lives mostly at Key West, Florida.

## 1929

William Faulkner publishes *The Sound and the Fury*.

## 1929–37

Great Depression in the United States, following the stock market crash of October 29, 1929.

## 1933

Eighteenth Amendment repealed (see 1917). President Franklin Roosevelt introduces the "New Deal," programs intended to end the Depression.

## 1935

Italy invades Ethiopia.

**1936–39**

Spanish Civil War.

**1936–37**

Writes, speaks, and raises money for Loyalists in Spanish Civil War.

**1937**

Japan invades China.

**1937–39**

In Spain covering civil war for North American Newspaper Alliance.

**1938**

Germany invades Austria.

**1939**

John Steinbeck publishes *The Grapes of Wrath.*

**1939–45**

World War II. The United States enters the war in 1941, after the December 7 Japanese attack on Pearl Harbor.

**1940**

Pauline Pfeiffer divorces him; he marries Martha Gellhorn.

**1941**

In China as war correspondent.

**1942–45**

Covers European theater of war as newspaper and magazine correspondent; also covers war in China, chases submarines in the Caribbean. Establishes Cuban residence in 1942.

**1944**

August 25—Allied liberation of Paris.

**1945**

May 7—Germany surrenders. August 15—Japan surrenders after the U.S. drops atomic bombs on Hiroshima and Nagasaki. World War II ends. December—Divorced from Martha Gellhorn.

**1946**

Marries Mary Welsh.

**1950–53**

Korean War; McCarthy era (Senator Joseph McCarthy holds hearings accusing many of being Communists; in 1954 he is condemned for his excesses by the U.S. Senate).

**1951**

J.D. Salinger publishes *The Catcher in the Rye.*

**1952**

Ralph Ellison publishes *Invisible Man.*

**1953**

Awarded the Pulitzer prize for *The Old Man and the Sea.*

**1954**

Wins Nobel prize for "forceful and style-making mastery of the art of modern narration."

**1961**

July 2—Dies of self-inflicted gunshot wound in his Ketchum, Idaho, home.

# WORKS BY ERNEST HEMINGWAY

*Three Stories and Ten Poems* (1923)

*in our time* (published privately by a small press in Paris) (1924)

*In Our Time* (first publication by a major American publisher; includes the stories from *Three Stories and Ten Poems*, the sketches from *in our time*, and new stories) (1925)

*The Torrents of Spring*; *The Sun Also Rises* (published as *Fiesta* in England) (1926)

*Men Without Women* (1927)

*A Farewell to Arms* (1929)

*Death in the Afternoon* (1932)

*Winner Take Nothing* (1933)

*Green Hills of Africa* (1935)

*To Have and Have Not* (1937)

*The Spanish Earth*; *The Fifth Column and the First Forty-Nine Stories* (1938)

*For Whom the Bell Tolls* (1940)

*Men at War* (edited by Hemingway) (1942)

*Across the River and into the Trees* (1950)

*The Old Man and the Sea* (1952)

## PUBLISHED POSTHUMOUSLY

*The Wild Years* (1962)

*A Moveable Feast* (1964)

*By-Line: Ernest Hemingway* (1967)

*The Fifth Column and Four Stories of the Spanish Civil War* (a new edition of the play and four previously uncollected stories) (1969)

*Islands in the Stream* (1970)

*The Nick Adams Stories* (includes some previously unpublished Adams material) (1972)

*Complete Poems* (1979)

*Ernest Hemingway: Selected Letters, 1917–1961*, edited by Carlos Baker (1981)

*The Dangerous Summer*; *Dateline: Toronto* (1985)

*The Garden of Eden* (1986)

# For Further Research

Roger Asselineau, ed., *The Literary Reputation of Hemingway in Europe*. New York: New York University Press, 1965.

John Atkins, *The Art of Ernest Hemingway: His Work and Personality*. London: Spring Books, 1952.

Carlos Baker, *Ernest Hemingway: A Life Story*. New York: Charles Scribner's Sons, 1969.

———, *Hemingway: The Writer as Artist*. Princeton, NJ: Princeton University Press, 1952.

Carlos Baker, ed., *Hemingway and His Critics: An International Anthology*. New York: Hill and Wang, 1961.

Sheridan Baker, *Ernest Hemingway: An Introduction and Interpretation*. New York: Holt, Rinehart & Winston, 1967.

Jackson J. Benson, *Hemingway: The Writer's Art of Self-Defense*. Minneapolis: University of Minnesota Press, 1969.

Jackson J. Benson, ed., *The Short Stories of Ernest Hemingway: Critical Essays*. Durham, NC: Duke University Press, 1975.

Denis Brian, *The True Gen*. New York: Grove Press, 1988.

Matthew J. Bruccoli, ed., *Ernest Hemingway: Cub Reporter*. Pittsburgh: University of Pittsburgh Press, 1970.

Peter Buckley, *Ernest*. New York: Dial Press, 1978.

Anthony Burgess, *Ernest Hemingway and His World*. New York: Charles Scribner's Sons, 1978.

Joseph DeFalco, *The Hero in Hemingway's Short Stories*. Pittsburgh: University of Pittsburgh Press, 1963.

Scott Donaldson, *By Force of Will: The Life and Art of Ernest Hemingway*. New York: New York Press, 1977.

Charles A. Fenton, *The Apprenticeship of Ernest Hemingway: The Early Years*. New York: Farrar, Straus, and Young, 1954.

Keith Ferrell, *Ernest Hemingway: The Search for Courage.* New York: M. Evans, 1984.

Norberto Fuentes, *Hemingway in Cuba.* Secaucus, NJ: Lyle Stuart, 1984.

Sheldon Norman Grebstein, *Hemingway's Craft.* Carbondale: Southern Illinois University Press, 1973.

Gregory H. Hemingway, *Papa: A Personal Memoir.* Boston: Houghton Mifflin, 1976.

Leicester Hemingway, *My Brother, Ernest Hemingway.* Cleveland: World, 1962.

Mary Welsh Hemingway, *How It Was.* New York: Knopf, 1976.

A.E. Hotchner, *Papa Hemingway: A Personal Memoir.* New York: Random House, 1966.

Richard R. Hovey, *Hemingway: The Inward Terrain.* Seattle: University of Washington Press, 1968.

Nicholas Joost, *Ernest Hemingway and the Little Magazines: The Paris Years.* Barre, MA: Barre Publishers, 1968.

Kenneth S. Lynn, *Hemingway.* New York: Simon & Schuster, 1987.

John K.M. McCaffery, ed., *Ernest Hemingway: The Man and His Work.* New York: Cooper Square Publishers, 1969.

James McLendon, *Papa: Hemingway in Key West 1928–1940.* Miami: E.A. Seamann, 1972.

James R. Mellow, *Hemingway: A Life Without Consequences.* Reading, MA: Addison-Wesley, 1992.

Jeffrey Meyers, *Hemingway: A Biography.* New York: Harper & Row, 1985.

Madelaine Hemingway Miller, *Ernie: Hemingway's Sister Sunny Remembers.* New York: Crown Publishers, 1975.

Constance Cappell Montgomery, *Hemingway in Michigan.* New York: Fleet, 1966.

James Nagel, ed., *Ernest Hemingway: The Writer in Context.* Madison: University of Wisconsin Press, 1984.

Michael S. Reynolds, *Hemingway's First War.* Princeton, NJ: Princeton University Press, 1976.

———, *The Young Hemingway.* New York: Basil Blackwell, 1986.

Lillian Ross, *Portrait of Hemingway.* New York: Simon & Schuster, 1961.

Marcelline Hemingway Sanford, *At the Hemingways: A Family Portrait.* Boston: Atlantic–Little Brown, 1962.

Samuel Shaw, *Ernest Hemingway.* New York: Frederick Ungar, 1973.

Edward F. Stanton, *Hemingway and Spain.* Seattle: University of Washington Press, 1989.

Robert O. Stephens, *Hemingway's Nonfiction: The Public Voice.* Chapel Hill, NC: Chapel Hill Press, 1968.

Henry Serrano Villard and James Nagel, *Hemingway in Love and War: The Lost Diary of Agnes von Kurowsky.* Boston: Northeastern University Press, 1989.

Linda Welshimer Wagner, ed., *Ernest Hemingway: Six Decades of Criticism.* East Lansing: Michigan State University Press, 1987.

Emily Stipes Watts, *Hemingway and the Arts.* Urbana: University of Illinois Press, 1971.

Robert P. Weeks, ed., *Hemingway: A Collection of Critical Essays.* Englewood Cliffs, NJ: Prentice-Hall, 1962.

Wirt Williams, *The Tragic Art of Ernest Hemingway.* Baton Rouge: Louisiana State University Press, 1981.

Philip Young, *Ernest Hemingway.* New York: Rinehart, 1952.

———, *Ernest Hemingway: A Reconsideration.* University Park: Pennsylvania State University Press, 1966.

## ONE MORE, SLIGHTLY ODDBALL, REFERENCE

One way to learn more about Hemingway's famous and much-imitated style is to read some "bad Hemingway." Comparing Hemingway imitators to the real thing can help illustrate why Hemingway's writing was the "true gen," as he might have put it. The reader might look for *The Best of Bad Hemingway* (New York: Harcourt Brace, 1989 and 1991), two volumes (so far) of entries from "The Harry's Bar & American Grill Imitation Hemingway Competition." To carry it a step further—to study the master by imitating him oneself . . . well, the contest rules are in the book.

# INDEX